Folksongs

&

Their Makers

FOLKSONGS AND THEIR MAKERS

Henry Glassie

Edward D. Ives

John F. Szwed

Bowling Green University Popular Press
Bowling Green, Ohio 43403

Library of Congress Card Catalogue number 79-137391

Copyright © by Bowling Green University Popular Press. Ray B. Browne, Editor. The Bowling Green University Popular Press is the publishing division of the Center for the Study of Popular Culture, Ray B. Browne, Director.

CONTENTS

Introduction: Folklore and Popular Culture   i

    Ray B. Browne

"Take That Night Train to Selma": An Excursion to the
Outskirts of Scholarship   1

    Henry Glassie

A Man and His Song: Joe Scott and "The Plain
Golden Band" 71

    Edward D. Ives

Paul E. Hall: A Newfoundland Song-Maker and
Community of Song. 149

    John F. Szwed

The Authors 168

Introduction

Folklore and Popular Culture

The relationship between folklore and popular culture is to many people unclear, and it is therefore debatable. On one extreme in the debate are those theorists who think that today's folklore was yesterday's popular culture. On the other extreme are those who believe that there is little direct relationship between the two. The truth, as usual, probably lies somewhere between.

The folklore that lasts is the creative acts of single individuals and the recreative acts of many persons—the mass of the folk. Larry Gorman, Woody Guthrie, and others of their kind, were creative geniuses who were of the folk. The material they created was from and of the folk, contained characteristics easily taken up and possessed by the folk. But these individuals were active creators. The mass of the folk, on the other hand, are passive recreators. The material they accept and recreate must be their kind of lore. They do not simply absorb indiscriminately the popular culture and recreate it in their own image. To a certain extent popular culture becomes so much a part of society at large and therefore so cliched that unwittingly the folk absorb it— through the pores, as it were. But such lore is once removed from popular culture. Generally, therefore, although much of the stimulus for the creation of folklore might come from popular culture or from the same sources popular culture comes from, folklore and popular culture are borne through similar but separate channels.

This is not to say, it should never be forgotten, that the two channels never have any intercommunication. Indeed they do. Jan Brunvand is perfectly accurate in seeing that there are in fact two kinds of *folklore* and one is exceeding close to popular culture: "Folklore$_1$ is what the professional folklorist is usually studying.... Folklore$_2$ is part of popular culture: those elements in culture that are *said* to have circulated traditionally in the past in oral or customary form among rural groups, but which in reality circulate only in printed or broadcast form in the mass media." And he quite properly adds that

Folklore$_2$ actually consists of two parts: "there is the perfectly valid idea of an old oral traditional group lore, and the mythical examples made up by publicists."

Because of the indefiniteness of the connection between folklore and popular culture the pioneer essays in this volume are especially timely and informative. Messrs. Hall and Scott were as near to the genuine folk tradition as we will find in contemporary society. They were members of a folk community, were stimulated by it, responded to it, were voices of it, and created their songs of the very stuff of the community. Mr. Weir is considerably different. His world has always been less a folk community than those of the two other men, more of a popular culture community. Although he was influenced by vestiges of folk life and activity in his community, he was more powerfully shaped by the popular forces in which he lived. His was a broader world—that of radio, television (he now owns a color set), newspaper, and visitors from the outside world. Yet if he is not a genuine member of an authentic folk community he is only half a step away, caught up in a transition which is altering all "folk" and "folk" communities—a transition which is changing the folk and their lore but not be any means eliminating them or it.

Mr. Weir is thus a profoundly important figure in the study of folklore and popular culture. Had he lived in an earlier and more authentic folk community, he would have been strictly a folk artist. But caught as he was in a community influenced by popular culture he created his songs from popular culture, just as the other two artists studied in this volume created their songs from the folk culture around them, and his songs then became folksongs. All three artists gathered their material from sources around them and then created songs which became genuine folksongs. The careers—and works—of all three are conclusive proof that popular culture does not automatically become folklore. These two streams in our society run parallel courses, and occasionally one stream mixes with the other—for short or long spans. But as Huck Finn and Jim knew about the confluence of the Mississippi River and the Ohio River below Cairo, Illinois, the two streams are distinguishable for a long time.

INTRODUCTION

The essay on Mr. Weir included in this volume was first published in the *Journal of Popular Culture*. When it was published there, both the author and the editor questioned the propriety of bringing it to light at that time. It was, however, felt then, as it is now, that such a trail-blazing study is too important in the understanding of individual artists and the creative processes of the folk in their milieu not to publish it.

The three studies in this volume, in the thoroughness and newness of their approach and coverage, bring new light to bear on the creative process, the sources and kinds of stimuli bearing on composition, the influences of artists' background and foreground. They are, therefore, both exciting and informative in their own right and are landmarks in the study of the creative process and the creator.

All of the tunes were autographed for this book by Dr. Norman Cazden, who also made the transcription for Paulie Hall's "Bachelor's Song." Our thanks to him.

Ray B. Browne

"TAKE THAT NIGHT TRAIN TO SELMA":
AN EXCURSION TO THE OUTSKIRTS OF SCHOLARSHIP

BY

HENRY GLASSIE

Dorrance Weir in June 1965

"Take that Night Train to Selma":
An Excursion to the Outskirts of Scholarship

by

Henry Glassie

If you were to ask for makers of traditional music at the green lit country bar and pool hall in Phoenix Mills, New York, the filling station at Fly Creek, the hotel in Oaksville, or at the hardscrabble farms which circle Christian Hill, run up Rum Hill and perch on Bed Bug Hill, you would be directed to the Weirs. Those who do not know that he has recently died will tell you to "look up Pop Weir"; those who do know will tell you that "you should've heard the old man play the violin" but that all of his nine (or seven or twelve) sons are musicians and that the Weirs' home near Oaksville, four and one-half miles northwest of Cooperstown, New York, would be about the only place in the area to hear "good old fashioned music."

Although they, naturally, all played baseball, not all of the nine Weir brothers took up instruments. Two of the boys, Donald and Les (called "Tad" because he was too young to fight in World War Two), and one of the girls, Buster, are fiddlers. Most of their tunes and techniques were learned from their father, though all play some Southern pieces brought to them by recordings, which Pop Weir, who called them "God damned rebel tunes," would play only begrudgingly. Like the faceless hillbillies on wax, the three second-generation fiddlers tend to play rapidly where Pop fiddled Northern style at a slow danceable pace; it was proper tempo which the old man emphasized most: if someone playing with him got off beat, he was apt to tap the offender with the fiddle bow. Pop Weir, who was born Elial Glen Weir in 1890, lived as a staunch Republican, and died just before his seventy-fifth birthday, was known as a fine fiddler outside of the area roughly twelve miles in diameter with Oaksville at its center where he played regularly for dances; once, dressed up as a cowboy, he performed on television.[1]

The singer and guitar player of the Weir clan is brother Dorrance, composer of the song at the core of this paper. Dorrance, a muscular man in his early forties, lived with his wife, Edie, and two sons, Butch and Wayne, in a home he built in "Cat Town" near Oaksville on the banks of Oak Creek across the road from his mother's house. Asked for an autobiography, Dorrance responded:

> When my youngest boy was born it cost
> me a hundred and sixty-five dollars, and when
> I was born it cost my father five dollars, so I don't
> know who's worth the most. And, today if you had
> a baby it would cost you pretty near four hundred
> dollars. Uncle Sam paid for Butch. But I was born
> in Philadelphia, New York, up in the northern
> part of the state, and we moved over to Hubbell
> Hollow. I don't know whether you've been
> there or not, you go beyond Whig Corners. . . ,
> it's ten miles from Cooperstown, an' go up in
> there on a dirt road and it's about—about
> where Christ kissed the hoot owl good bye.
> An' my father used to be a fiddler, an' he would
> go to these house parties an' so forth and fiddle,
> an' they'd take up a collection about eleven

o'clock at night. He'd get a dollar an' a half
or two dollars or something an' they'd feed a
big meal, an' then he'd fiddle for a couple of
more hours an' come home; hook up the
horses. I remember this, and I always used
to envy anyone that could play an instrument;
I thought it was the most wonderful thing to see
someone. When I was in the second grade
we moved to Richfield Springs and at Christmas
time I had caught a muskrat and I sold it an'
I got two dollars and a quarter, I think, for it.
And, my mother let me have the quarter;
the two dollars went for a pair of boots or
something. But I took the quarter and I
bought a tin fiddle in a five-and-dime store.
And they wouldn't let me keep it. I had to
take it back because twenty-five cents was
quite a lot of money. So finally in about nineteen thirty-one my father bought a tenor
banjo for sixteen dollars and my mother
was the most put out woman in the world. O,
it was a beautiful instrument! I started peckin'
on it—no instructions or anything—an' I got so
I could play the G and the C chord on it, but
never well. Finally we moved to the home-place
here in nineteen thirty-six an' I bought a guitar,
strings about that far off the finger board, an'
I started peckin' around on it. I didn't have
any instructions or nothing; I just pecked at it
and would put my fingers where the chords were
or where they weren't until it sounded right to
me, and that's where I learned. Then my brother
Donald took up the fiddle at the same time and
we used to go in the what-they-called the parlor
and play nights. Then he went into the service
an' I went in the service; he took a fiddle and I

> took a guitar. An' when we came home,
> why, this is what become of us. But still my
> father was—people would come from miles
> around to hear my father fiddle. He was pretty
> good.[2]

Most of Dorrance's brothers are carpenters or teamsters who have moved northward to the classically named cities of the Mohawk Valley. Of those left in the hilly country around Oaksville, Dorrance is the best known musician. His music, good humor, and handsome wife bring him invitations to many of the house parties thrown by members of three of the socio-economic groups in the area: the lower middle-class shopkeepers and blue-collar workers, the numerically dominant poor rural workers, and the intellectual personnel who make nearby Cooperstown "the Village of Museums." These parties are set up specifically for music-making; the evening alternates between roughly half hour periods of music and talk, the women talking about women not present, the men in another part of the room, in a different room, or outside in good weather, drinking, talking money, politics or music, and telling jokes. Dorrance is the center of the musical periods. He stands with the other members of the make shift-band around him, and smiles, plays and sings to the accompaniment, generally, of one or two fiddles, a harmonica and "bones," pieces of smooth hardwood clacked together in time. Occasional requests for tunes or songs come from the attentive, predominantly female audience seated on the other side of the room, or from within the usually all male band. Most of the numbers performed are selected by Dorrance; it is he who decides the key in which they are to be played and it is he who provides them with any verbal introductions.

The songs he sings have a variety of sources. Some were learned from his father ("The Kerry Recruit,"[3] "Wal, I Swan,"[4] or "Gold Top Walking Cane"[5]); many more came from the recordings of Country artists like Vernon Dalhart, Lulu Belle and Scotty, or Johnny Cash ("The Wreck of the Number Nine,"[6] or "I Won't Go Hunting With You Jake,"[7] which is a great local favorite because of the hound baying imitation provided by his wife). Because he listens to the radio in an area not served by a full-time Country Music station and has two teen-age sons, he has heard and absorbed some of the products of the popular folknik revival. His heterogeneous repertoire also includes some of the bawdy songs, such as "The Winnipeg Whore"[8] and an obscene parody of "Put On Your Old Grey Bonnet," which seem to be known to most of the men who slogged through the Second World War. He plays, too, a great number of square dance tunes, which are old in central New York tradition, either as melodic instrumentals or as chordal accompaniment for a fiddler or his own singing calls.[9]

The songs he sang at a small party attended by three middle-class, middle-age couples in Cooperstown, are typical of his fare:[10] "Jack and Joe," "MacNamara's Band," "The Old Ninety-Seven," "The Wreck of the Number Nine," both the song and singing square dance call for "Golden Slippers" and "Nellie Gray," "O Susannah" and "Camptown Races" (two songs identified as the work of Stephen Foster and triggered by "Nellie Gray" which he said was also a Foster tune), "Beer Barrel Polka," "Marching Through Georgia," "She'll Be Comin' Round the Mountain," "The Isle of Capri," "This Land Is Your Land," the singing call for "The Girl I Left Behind Me," "Pistol Packin' Momma," "On Top of Old Smoky," "Old Dan Tucker," "Old Zip Coon," "West Texas Town of El Paso"(announced as a Marty Robbins song), "East Virginia Blues," "The Strawberry Roan," "Wolverton Mountain," "The Gold Top Walking Cane," "You are My Sunshine" (written, he said, by "some guy that sang himself to the governor of Louisiana"), "Old Mountain Dew," "You're a Little Too Young, My Boy," "Great Speckled Bird," "Bringing in the Sheaves," "Gotta Travel On," "Peg Leg Jack," "Hard Travelin'," "The Banks of the Ohio," "Bury Me Beneath the Willow," "Please Mr. Truman" (sung to the melody of "Lily Marlene," this is a plea to be allowed to return stateside and "Let the boys at home see Rome"), "You Gotta Walk That Lonesome Valley," "Leave the Dishes in the Sink, Aub," (on which there will be more below), "Wildwood Flower," "Why Did I Get Married," "Just a Lonely Cowboy," "The Prisoner's Song," "Gimme That Old Time Religion," "Jesse James." And, twice he sang "Take That Night Train to Selma."

"Take That Night Train to Selma" was first heard at house

parties in the Oaksville-Toddsville-Cooperstown area in March of 1965. Through that spring it regularly consisted of these stanzas; the first one serving as a chorus, the second and third always appearing in the order they are given here.[11]

1. Take that night train to Selma,
   And here's another thing:
   You could be ridin'
   Next to Martin Luther King.

2. The wops had Mussolini,
   And then they lost the war,
   And then they joined the niggers,
   And they joined up with CORE.

3. So every night
   You can hear them dagoes sing,
   "I pledge allegiance
   To old Martin Luther King."

As the song was sung minor variation was constant. He often sang "may" rather than "could" in the third line of the first stanza; the last line of that stanza was altered and became fixed as, "Right side Martin Luther King." The second line of the second stanza began on occasion with "That's why" or "Of course" instead of "And then." The third line of the second stanza might begin with, "So now" rather than "And then," and the last line at different times was: "And they all belong to CORE," or "They're all signed up with CORE." The last three lines of the third stanza did not change (except for the infrequent insertion of "sure" between "I" and "pledge" in the third line) but the first one changed quickly to "And early every evening."

When sung, "Take That Night Train to Selma" is not only less ugly than it is on paper, its confusing content is minimized. His diverse audience was amused by it, recognizing it only as vaguely anti-Italian and anti-Negro. The first stanza tells the listener to ride next to a Negro on a southbound train. In mentioning Martin Luther King,

Dorrance intended a topical reference to the Selma march. He also utilized Dr. King's name as a symbol for all Negroes; once he referred to a group of black men on whom he and some friends played a trick as "migrant workers who happened to have Martin Luther King skin on." Stanzas two and three indicate that the Italians have joined the Negroes in their struggle for their rights. These first unclear stanzas are enmeshed in the song's birth in the late winter of 1965 which Dorrance describes in two interviews:

A

I was in Rochester and there's quite a colored element up there, an' the white boys didn't appreciate it, you know, I mean, really, they didn't go with it. An' we had this short, fat, lazy guinea working for us, and my partner an' I would holler to him an'—no response. We couldn't get any help from him, so. . .Old Tom said, "You better go to Selma." That's how it started. He said, "You'll make out better down there with your companions." An' this song "Take That Night Train to Memphis," I Just thought," Take That Night Train to Selma." And then I had to get something in there about the Italians, so that's when I said, "the wops had Mussolini an' that's why they lost the war an' so now they joined the niggers an' all belong to CORE'" An' that really [laughs]. An' I had several that I've forgotten. It's simple, easy to make those, up, you could do that, you know that. And that's the way it started.

H.G.   Did that Italian guy particularly like colored guys?

Dorrance Weir: O, no. No. He hated them, an' I was gettin' through to him. It was a real sharp needle, see, an' so that's why I did it. He was lazy. But, I could jab him that way.[12]

B

> I was workin' in Rochester. An' the colored element there is almost two to one—in Rochester, New York! An' we had this little Italian. He was a laborer on the job workin' for us. And he was always giving us the needle about something. And so, I always used to make up little rhymes and so forth about him. So I started in one day and I was thinking an' I said (I was thinking of Selma, Alabama) and I said—I was singing to him, "Take the night train to Selma and here's another thing an' you may be ridin' right side Martin Luther King." And I thought, gosh, I gotta get to him harder than that or it won't bother him. An' it didn't. That didn't bother him a bit, so I thought—'course I have to get through to someone—so I said, I thought for awhile, an' I said, "The wops had Mussolini. An' that's why they lost the war. So then they joined the niggers and now they belong to CORE, then early every evening you can hear them dagoes sing, 'I pledge allegiance to old Martin Luther King.'" [laughs]. I thought that was real good. None of the rest come out as good as that.[13]

The first stanzas, composed to taunt a laborer of Italian descent, provided the core of the song, but in singing to an audience 135 miles from Rochester, unaware of the song's origin (he never told its story publicly), and concerned more with the Negro's stride toward freedom than a specific clash of personalities, Dorrance needed new stanzas. The first to join the original three was an additional simple chorus:

> 4. Take that night train to Selma.
> Take that night train to Selma.
> Take that night train to Selma.
> To Selma, Alabam.

In the late spring two new stanzas were added to the song which were unrelated to the notion of sending the Italian to Selma. These are comments on integration, the government's attitude toward it, and Mr. Weir's attitude toward both. The "you" has shifted from direct reference to the laborer to an impersonal and plural you. Like stanzas two and three, he treated these as a pair, usually singing them in this order:

5. Take that night train to Selma;
   Make that your destination,
   If you believe
   In this damned integration.

6. Take that night train to Selma,
   Selma, Alabam,
   And you will be pleasing
   Good old Uncle Sam.

He occasionally sang the last word of stanza five as "segregation," not through any liberal lapse, but only in error. Sometimes in stanza six, Uncle Sam is considered "dear" rather than "good."

At a party near Oaksville on June 17, 1965, he sang the song twice. The first time, it was composed of the stanzas above in 5-6-2 3-1 order. The second singing included three new stanzas. Two—seven and eight—were composed during a break in the music; stanza nine was invented while he continued to strum the guitar through the laughter which followed stanza eight.

7. The white man brought'em over;
   They brought 'em as a slave.
   They said that they could stay here,
   Stay here as a slave.

8. We'll send 'em back to Africa.
   Wouldn't do any harm
   If they took a dago
   Under each arm.

9. But we'll keep'em,
   No matter how you figger,
   And they are nothin'
   But a big black nigger.

After stanza nine there was no laughter, save a sarcastic ha-ha-ha by his wife; that stanza was never sung again. The well received stanzas seven and eight were reworked that night into a pair which became a standard ingredient of the song:

7. The white man brought them over;
   He brought them as a slave.
   He said they could stay here
   As long as they behaved.

8. But now, we'll send them back to Africa.
   Wouldn't do any harm
   If they take a dago
   Under each arm.

While singing he occasionally forgot lines and recomposed on the spot with such rapidity that a person who had never heard the song before would not be able to recognize any mistake. Once in the late fall of 1965 he compressed stanzas seven and eight thus:

The white man brought the niggers,
They couldn't do any harm.
Now they'll send 'em back to Africa
With a wop under each arm.

As local interest increased in Dorrance's song, he was commonly greeted with the question, "any new ones?" He tried to oblige his audience; about the first of July he composed three new stanzas:

10. A nigger goes to Selma,
    And his skin is black;

>   It's heaven for the nigger,
>   'Cause he ain't comin' back.
>
> 11. The niggers want everything;
>   You can't do 'em any favors,
>   Or else they'll cut you
>   With that long black razor.
>
> 12. The white man says, "You-all";
>   The black man says, "Yes sir,"
>   And I can't figger out
>   Which one talks like the other.

Stanzas ten and eleven were soon forgotten and are preserved only because Mrs. Weir wrote them down for me the night they were composed at a party. Dorrance never wrote down any of the song; it was composed and kept entirely in his head. He remembered stanza twelve, however, and although it never elicited much reaction from his audience, he sang it occasionally because he has been in the South and the Southern accent—the question of whether the white Southerner's accent is like that of the Negro or vice versa—intrigues him:

> I wonder where that Southern accent came from.
> That would be something to go back to, you know,
> and do a little research on. The nigger brought it
> over and the white man took it [chuckles].[14]

Sitting in the modern kitchen of the Weirs' home on the evening of July 9, 1965, his son, Butch, suggested that there should be something about Abraham Lincoln in the song. Dorrance immediately composed stanza thirteen; within five minutes stanzas fourteen and fifteen followed.

> 13. Lincoln was the president;
>   He started the Civil War;
>   And now it has dwindled down,
>   And they call it CORE.

14. The Yankees fought the rebels
    In the Civil War.
    Now they should band together,
    And all fight CORE.

15. The black man worked for the white man;
    Everybody was happy then.
    But, that integratin' Abie
    Started something that will never end.

After singing these stanzas he commented that his grandfather fought in the Union army, but that if he had known what Negroes were like he would not have fought to free them. Although his family found stanza fourteen amusing and encouraged him to retain it, he was uninterested and never sang any of these historical stanzas again.

Requests for "Take That Night Train to Selma" continued but in the late summer and through the fall of 1965, he composed no new stanzas. In January 1966, I asked Dorrance about his song:

H.G.: I haven't seen you since August. Have you made up any new verses?

Dorrance Weir: No, I'm workin' on another song, but I wouldn't dare reveal any part of this song because immediately you'd be a millionaire. . . . It's a protest song, but nothing to do with race. No, it's a protest song but it's between man and wife. There's always protest there.

H.G.: Why haven't you made up any new verses?

Dorrance Weir: Really, I'm not concerned about the integration or segregation or any part of it. There's been no one around that I could throw a needle into. I have to have someone around that I can abuse, you might say. . . . When it doesn't bother 'em I get no kick out of it, so I— I get no kick out of it.

H.G.: After you left Rochester, when you were here, who were you making fun of?

Dorrance Weir: Well, my wife wanted just some more verses to the song, so you could sit down and write a million of 'em. Have to please the boss you know.[15]

Although he said in January that work on the song was over, he composed three new stanzas in the summer of 1966:

16. O, the rebels knew the story,
    That's why they fought the war.
    If they'd a won it,
    There wouldn't be any CORE.

17. They rioted in Rochester,
    And in Chicago too.
    It's gettin' so a white man
    Don't know what to do.

18. We give them everything they want,
    And still they want more.
    And if we do not come across,
    They all run to CORE.

The sixteenth stanza, apparently a reworking of number fourteen which he had not sung for a year, was sung once in the first week of July when stanza seventeen was sung four times; in one rendition the "And" was omitted from the beginning of the second line. Within a month, stanza eighteen, which is reminiscent of discarded stanza eleven, had joined number seventeen producing a pair sung regularly in the song. An interview in August, 1966, after he had sung the song three times at a party in his home and tape-recorded it once in 5-6-2-3-5-1-17-18-5-6-7-8-1 order, follows:

H.G.: At Christmas time you said you weren't going to

make up any new verses. Then you have two new ones. Why'd you start making them up again?

Dorrance Weir: Well, I heard about this big march an' the riots an' I thought, there's another one right there. And there's another one; Martin Luther King got hit with a rock. There's another verse there. One of these days I'll come up with it.[16]

At the beginning of 1966, Dorrance Weir had begun to lose interest in "Take That Night Train to Selma." It had been half a year since he had composed any new stanzas and he did not feel that any more would be forthcoming. The song amounted to a presentation of his attitudes and as such it was sufficient. The riot in Rochester, however brought racial strife close to him, and it inspired new stanzas (17 and 18) with which Dorrance began to comment on national events; his seventeenth stanza refers to the July 1966 disorders in Chicago as well as to those in Rochester, where the song had begun. In its shift from a general statement to a statement on specific events, the song moved still farther in the anti-Negro direction, and it was provided with new material and potential. The drama of events increased during the following two years (as did the scholastic and social need for studies of WASP culture and racism—one had to read only the daily paper and the Kerner Commission Report). I assumed that Dorrance's song had continued to grow, and when the chance presented itself, I took a trip to central New York.

The first friend that I met on the drizzly morning of September 11, 1968, told me that Dorrance had made up "a new verse" after the assassination of Martin Luther King. I drove to the school where he was working and interrupted Dorrance who was at work with an electric drill. We talked about his recent troubles for awhile; he agreed to meet me that night and I left. As I crossed the muddy parking lot, Dorrance walking swiftly behind me, called out for me to stop. He stood in his soft khaki uniform, his apron of nails around his waist, and gestured as Dorrance always gestures—tightly, with his shoulders square, his elbows pressed against his sides, hard palms turned out—

and said, "Hey, Hank, I finally finished that 'Night Train to Selma.' I've put the finishing touches on it." He turned to go, looked back and grinning said, "I was waiting for them to shoot him."

That night a few friends sat around a generous Cooperstown parlor. Dorrance had brought his guitar, its finish bleached off in last winter's snow, through the rain and he was prevailed upon to set his drink down and sing. He stood and sang and played "The Wildwood Flower," "Old Mountain Dew," "The Old Gray Bonnet," "Bury Me Beneath the Willow," "Why Did I Get Married," "Chinese Breakdown" and "Ragtime Annie" (instrumentals), "Gotta Travel On," "The Gold Top Walking Cane," "You're a Little Too Young, My Boy," "Your Cheating Heart," "When You and I Were Young Maggie," "Dust On the Bible," "Pistol Packin' Momma," "Please Mr. Truman," "You Gotta Walk that Lonesome Valley," "Jesse James," "Golden Slippers," "Frankie and Johnny," and we tape-recorded the "final" version of "Take That Night Train to Selma:"

5. Take that night train to Selma;
   Make that your destination,
   If you want to believe
   In this damned integration.

6. Take that night train to Selma,
   Selma, Alabam,
   And you will be pleasin'
   Your dear Old Uncle Sam.

2. The wops had Mussolini,
   That's why they lost the war,
   And then they joined the niggers,
   And they all belong to CORE.

3. And early every evening
   You can hear them dagoes sing,
   "I pledge allegiance
   To old Martin Luther King."

1. Take that night train to Selma,
   And here's another thing:
   You won't be seated
   Next to Martin Luther King.

19. They brought 'em from the jungle,
    Tried to make men from the apes,
    But all they do is riot,
    Plunder, and rape.

17. They rioted in Rochester,
    And in Chicago too.
    O, it's gettin' so a white man
    Don't know what to do.

18. We give them everything they want,
    And still they want more.
    If they don't get it,
    They all run to CORE.

5. Take that night train to Selma;
   Make that your destination,
   If you want to believe
   In this damned integration.

6. Take that night train to Selma,
   To Selma, Alabam,
   And you will be pleasin'
   Dear old Uncle Sam.

20. They shot him down in Memphis,
    Memphis, Tennessee.
    He was preachin' 'bout the white folks,
    Guys like you and me.

21. And the wops, they went in mournin';

O, how they cried;
O, just to think their savior,
Dear old Martin Luther died.

22. But they ought to hang a medal
On the guy that pulled the trigger.
'Cause he made another
Damned good nigger.

5. Take that night train to Selma,
Make that your destination,
If you want to believe
In this damned integration.

1. Take that night train to Selma,
And here's another thing;
You won't be seated
Right side Martin Luther King.

23. O, they dragged him to the graveyard
Behind a train of mules.
I guess when they bury a nigger,
That's the standard rule.

24. And they think they've caught his killer
In a foreign country.
And they're bringin' him back
To the land of liberty.

25. But they'll never convict him,
Not in all creation;
All he's got to do
Is plead discrimination.

5. Take that Night train to Selma;
Make that your destination.

>   If you want to believe
>   In this damned integration.
>
> 6. Take that night train to Selma,
>   Selma, Alabam,
>   You will be pleasin'
>   Your dear old Uncle Sam.

After he had finished and the light laughter had subsided, Dorrance said that he had forgotten some of the song; he referred to stanza eight and sang:

> 26. And during all the riots,
>   To those who know the score,
>   O, the first thing they break in to
>   Is a liquor store.

In the two years since I had seen him, change in the song had been great. Alterations had been made in the text which were minor matters of taste and refinement: "seated" instead of "riding" in the third line of stanza three, the words "want to" inserted into the third line of five to improve its scansion, a similar lengthening of the last line of the sixth stanza, and a new third line for stanza eighteen making its construction smoother.

Dorrance and his audience agreed that stanza nineteen, which had not been recorded before, was not new and that it probably dated to the summer of 1966 when stanzas seventeen and eighteen, which also deal with the riots, were composed.

Old Tom, who was working in Rochester with Dorrance when the first stanzas of "Night Train to Selma" erupted, had said once that someone would shoot Martin Luther King someday. When Dorrance heard the news he was not surprised, and he composed two new stanzas (20 and 21) at a party held the night after the assassination, which would be April 5, 1968. At the same time he changed "could" to "won't" in the third line of the first stanza. While singing stanza one, he emphasizes this change with a small smile and instrumental punctuation.

Stanzas Twenty through twenty-six are all immediately linked to the events surrounding the assassination of Dr. King: the murder itself (20), the disturbances which followed the murder (26), the funeral (23), and the capture of James Earl Ray in England (24). The historic details are accurate, and taken together these stanzas provide a loose account of a national tragedy not unlike the blues ballad on the assassination of McKinley which survives in tradition, although the parallels are accidental. New stanzas came rapidly during the period following the assassination; the last new stanza before the murder had been composed about twenty months earlier. As with the initial set of stanzas in the song, Dorrance was most pleased with the first stanzas in the assassination series. He enjoyed stanzas twenty and particularly twenty-one; hearing the latter played back, he said with a smile, "I like that." In the terms of the song, these are the most conservative stanzas: twenty-one continues the theme of stanzas two and three; stanza twenty used stanza six as a model, and, farther, it involved a bizarre logic of the type frequently employed—to compound the irony— by Black Muslims, for the song Dorrance used in developing his song was "Night Train to Memphis." When he first composed stanza twenty-three, it had read "team" rather than "train of mules." Even as modified, he was not pleased with that stanza and as the tape played back he shook his head negatively and remarked, "There ought to be somethin' following that up."

The new stanzas are continuous with those of the past. Formally they are the same, and humor (stanzas 25 and 26) and the notion at the song's source (stanza 21) can still be found in them. But the new stanzas, those cued by national events (17 through 26), have become increasingly political, increasingly bitter. The song's message has become progressively clearer (Dorrance felt the song could be completed after the death of Dr. King; any event concerning the worker of Italian heritage would have been irrelevant). This is the result of more than the internal drift of the song as it has been modeled into an anti-Negro statement; its tone as well as its content has been influenced by the recent events to which Dorrance and his audiences have reacted with more and more anger. The song has become part of the terrifying American mood of the period which has followed the twitch of conscience caused by the murder of Dr. King. Dorrance sang that "they ought to hang a medal on the guy" who killed the man who had been "preachin' 'bout the white folks, guys like you and me" at the same time that white policemen were murdering black political leaders in cold blood, that the Wallace for president movement (supported on bumper stickers and posters throughout Dorrance's hills) surged, driving even "liberal" candidates into advocating the insidiously racist issue of "law and order." The demonstrations in 1970 by the "hard hat" construction workers were no surprise to people who were willing to talk to bright and perceptive, if sadly prejudiced, people like Dorrance years before the Administration's "Southern Strategy," claiming the support of the nonexistent "silent majority," had resulted in the divisive policies which are currently tearing the nation apart.

II

In all of the contexts in which Dorrance normally performed, he sang his song in the same way. In all of the contexts the song received the same response—laughter.

In the last week of October, 1965, he packed his guitar as well as his rifle and sleeping bag up to a hunting camp in the Adirondacks. At night while the others, weary from the day's deer stalking, drank, played cards and cleaned their rifles, Dorrance played and sang. The group—a salesman, a surveyor, a realtor, and a veterinarian, all from near Cooperstown—thought "Take That Night Train to Selma" was a "real corker" and requested it often.[17]

In many of our conversations on traditional music, Dorrance mentioned Ken Kane, who, he said, was "a real character." Kane casually worked a small farm, and, though he did not hold a steady job, he was a skilled mechanic, electrician, and stone mason. He played the guitar, melodeon ("button accordion"), concertina, ukulele, harmonica ("mouth organ"), piano, and he continued to play the fiddle regularly for square dances with Levant Rathbun, a guitar playing stone mason who had occasionally accompanied Pop Weir. On the night of July 9, 1965, Mr. and Mrs. Weir and I bought some beer at the Oaksville hotel and drove over the dark gravel roads to Kane's farm on Christian Hill.

Kane's home, a clapboarded Greek Revival cottage in need of paint, was typical of the older homes in the area and stood as a symbol of the cultural connections between upstate New York and New England.[18] The back wall of the parlor had been knocked out merging it with the kitchen. A low bed was shoved near the remaining interior partition; behind this Kane's six year old son hid; on it reclined Kane's brother, Leon, a plumber, who held a guitar during most of the evening but was not asked to join in the music making because he played "by note" and could not keep up. In the front of the room, between the windows which stared out at the road, a television stood, flanked by bookcases which held few books, some popcorn, instrument cases, and all manner of electrical jetsam. On the walls, pictures of birds snipped from magazines were pasted and a shellacked rack held rifles and shotguns. Two guitars and a fiddle were piled next to the stuffed chair in the corner where Ken Kane sat. Alice, his oldest daughter who was to be married in a few weeks, his wife Rose, and Mrs. Weir sat on chairs placed in a row oddly near the center of the room. His youngest daughter, Hilda, spent most of the night on the porch talking to a boyfriend on the telephone, the cord of which was stretched taut around the door jamb. Dorrance sat down in a chair opposite Kane's and listened while he told of the tricks he had played on a neighbor, "a stingy old bastard who wouldn't pay a nickel to see Christ ride a bicycle up a two inch pipe."[19] He talked, too, about the times he used to go to Pop Weir's store to play with him; he greatly admired Pop's fiddling, especially of the jigs and reels, which Pop loved to play, and he felt that Pop's sons fiddled too fast. Dorrance asked him "to play a little something for us." He tuned up a tenor guitar, which he had amplified because he was a little hard of hearing, and played "Marching Through Georgia,"[20] picking the melody with his fingers alone because his thumb was "curled up" as a result of a shotgun accident. Kane had taught his daughter to play the guitar (she used the same incomplete and slightly dissonant G chord that he did), and after his instrumental he asked her to play and sing. This she was reluctant to do. Dorrance offered to sing with her, and her father said she should do it because "it's not everyday you get to play with somebody as good as Dorrance Weir." Kane went upstairs and fetched the guitar he had constructed for her out of pieces of other guitars and decorated with red and green glass motorcycle reflectors, and she went into her bedroom and returned with the notebooks into which she had copied the lyrics of many popular songs. With Dorrance's assistance she sang part of "Silver Threads and Golden Needles"[21] in hillbilly soprano; after it Ken Kane snorted that he did not like these "newfangled songs." He and Dorrance then played "Yankee Doodle" and "Willow Tree."[22] Despite prodding, Kane was unwilling to sing, but a beer later he sang, accompanying himself on the guitar:

My wife she run with a different kind,
An' often goes out on a spree,
And she leaves me behind, the baby to mind,
An' yodel um, a doodle um dee.
Yodel-a-e-o, 'dl-a-e-o, 'dl-a-ee.[23]

While he was singing Kane snickered and, when the song was ended, all laughed. Dorrance, smiling, stood up in front of his chair, bent forward from the waist, his right forearm bracing the guitar against his body, and, without looking directly at anyone, he sang:

Take that night train to Selma,
To Selma, Alabam,
An' you will be pleasin'
Good ol' Uncle Sam.

That night train to Selma,
An' here's another thing;
O, you could be ridin'
Right side Martin Luther King.

Take that night train to Selma;
Make that your destination,
If you believe
In this damned integration.

The wops had Mussolini;
That's why they lost the war,
So, now they join the niggers,
An' they all belong to CORE.

Then early every evening
You can hear them dagoes sing,
"I pledge allegiance
To old Martin Luther King."

The white man brought'em over,
Brought'em as a slave.

O, he said that **they** could stay here
As long as they behave.

But we'll send 'em back to Africa;
Won't do any harm.
We'll send them back
With a wop under each arm.

Take that night train to Selma,
Take that night train to Selma,
Take that night train to Selma,
To Selma, Alabam.[24]

While there was music, the listeners were still and silent; as soon as the song ended, Ken Kane guffawed, Leon grinned broadly, Mrs. Kane, her arms tightly folded, smiled and then chuckled, Dorrance, smiling and gesturing with his guitar said, "there's alot of verses we didn't do." After a pause for another beer, Kane played dance tunes on the fiddle (which he had electrified because, he said, it is hard to play for three hours at a dance on an unamplified instrument) while Dorrance and Alice followed him on guitars. The talk swung primarily on encounters with Negroes. Kane was amused by the fact that he enjoyed eating soup out of the can despite the fact that it had probably been prepared by "some old nigger woman," and Dorrance recounted some of the tricks he and his buddies had played on black workers. With midnight it became time to go; Dorrance stood in the door singing "Gotta Travel On,"[25] and Ken Kane, who was scraping away in accompaniment, said he was "better than anything you could hear on TV." Mrs. Kane walked out to the truck with Mrs. Weir, Kane accompanied Dorrance and me, laughing and singing *sotto voce* a snatch of an obscene parody of the "Prisoner's Song."[26] He invited us back saying, "I haven't had so much fun since my wife caught her left tit in the wringer."

While he realized that most of the college educated museum people he knew did not agree with him on the "race business," Dorrance brought the "Night Train to Selma" out at their parties and it was generally greeted with the same laughter that it was in Ken Kane's old farmhouse. There was only one of his acquaintances in the museum circle to whom Dorrance did not wish to sing the song; he considered this socially concerned man a "nigger lover" who would be blind to the song's humor. Nevertheless, when chance finally brought them together at a museum party in Cooperstown in October, 1965, Dorrance, after a series of fiddle tunes, announced:

> This is a nigger story [the party's hubbub continues].
> Wait! [whistles]. You've got to listen to this [the crowd becomes quiet; he strums the guitar and sings]:

> Take that night train to Selma,
> And here's another thing:
> You may be riding
> Right side Martin Luther King.

> The wops had Mussolini,
> Of course they lost the war,
> So then, they joined the niggers
> And now they belong to **CORE**.

> And early every evening
> You can hear them dagoes sing,
> "I pledge allegiance
> To old Martin Luther King."

At this point the song was interrupted by great laughter, especially that of N.L., who said, "Wonderful. Any more verses to that?" Mrs. Weir replied, "There are about twenty verses, but he's forgotten them. And he'll sing that one verse and then burst out laughing." Said N.L., "I don't blame him."[27]

"Take That Night Train to Selma" was acceptable to the Cooperstown deer hunters who represent the small town upstate New York middle class, to Ken Kane's family who represent the economically depressed rural population attempting to live much as people lived when Dorrance's father was a young man, and even to the predominantly liberal museum people. The deer hunters responded to the song partially as anti-Italian, and by logical extension anti-Catholic, but most others considered it a comment on the current place and action of the Negro; it was racial prejudice with which his audiences, whether progressive or reactionary, were most concerned. To those who agreed with his prejudices, the song was acceptable as a statement of shared attitudes—an expression of culture. To those who did not hold his prejudices, its acceptability lay in the fact that in all contexts the good humor of its presentation outweighed its specific message. The confusing—unexpected, comprehensible but not understandable—nature of the song, the result of its unknown origin, seemed to assist in the maintenance of the song's primary effect as humorous—exactly the characteristic which separates it from the action oriented 'protest song" of picket line and coffee house.[28]

The song, called "Dorrance's song" by most people, was acceptable to his audiences, too, because they had a hand in its composition. The artist's judgment, the brooding which brings him to delete the bad and encourage the good during creation (what Ben Shahn calls his "inner critic"[29] and what William Faulkner means when he says, "the writer...has got to be a censor"[30]), was externalized in the making of "Take That Night Train to Selma." The involvement of the audience in the creative act (all of his stanzas were composed with others present) resulted from his limited practice as a creator and the cultural complexity of his intellectual environment. If the creator and his audience are members of a human aggregate sharing attitudes, aesthetics and experiences, he can, as Larry Gorman did in the lumber camps[31] or as John Updike did in the pages of *The New Yorker*, present completed a predictably acceptable work of art. Traveling among people whose cultures were different, in some instances nearly as different as America will bear, Dorrance had to be acutely sensitive to his audience. His audience continually urged him to create new stanzas and even suggested subject matter to him (stanzas 13-15). After the composition of each new stanza it was presented in a performance of the whole song to his audience. Generally, if it received the correct reaction—laughter—it was retained in the song (stanzas 7 and 8, for example); if sour or blank looks followed the new stanza, it was eliminated (stanza 9). There was, in addition, a personal element in the process, for one stanza which was never well received was occasionally employed because it interested him (stanza 12), although it never did become integral to the song. And, a few stanzas which were well received did not particularly amuse him and were discarded (stanza 14, for example). However, all of the stanzas which became a standard part of the song were well received when initially presented, and none of those which his audience disliked became standard. His audience dictated the general direction of the song toward a greater concern with the Negro. As it grew Dorrance regarded it more and more as a comment on race relations and its content became increasingly anti-Negro (stanzas 2 and 3 are primarily anti-Italian, secondarily anti-Negro; stanzas 7 and 8 are primarily anti-Negro, secondarily anti-Italian; stanzas 17 and 18 are only anti-Negro). His audience, further, maintained a broad control over its content which acted to prevent it from becoming a totally personal statement and to keep it acceptable; specifically, his audience rejected the most stereotypic and directly offensive of the stanzas (9, 10, 11, the last of which re-entered the song in a milder form as stanza 18) because, on the whole, his audience was less prejudiced, less violent than he.

III

Creative people like Dorrance Weir are uncommon in European-American communities like his, which include among the traits of their culture some of importance which—from the standpoint of the great society, the nation—veer away from the mass and public norm in the direction of "tradition"—traits with which the adjective "folk" can be legitimately associated. Consideration of oral literary forms generally emphasize change; too often they compare the folksong's many texts, none of them the correct one, with the single acceptable text of the art song—the variability of one with the fixedness of the other.[32] This is the story the compilations of song and tale texts tell. Yet, the usual folksinger is no more creative than the usual performer of pop or art song; both share in the Western tradition of the performer as repeater, of the performer as distinct from the audience during performance so that the performance amounts to a presentation requiring authority. He is true to his source, taking pride in the fact that the song is being sung as it was when he learned it. With varying degrees of success he attempts to hold the song steady. In May, 1962, for example, Ruby Bowman Plemmons, a government secretary living near the Capitol in the District of Columbia, sang five ballads which she had learned from her mother as a young girl at the crest of the Blue Ridge,[33] and which had been recorded from her three months less than thirty years before by A.K. Davis and included in his *More Traditional Ballads of Virginia*.[34] When the old and new texts were compared it was found that she had remembered three more incremental stanzas and a repetitive line, but that out of 276 lines she had made changes in only twenty. Of these changes, one was conscious;[35] the balance were minor: a sea was described as "foamy" instead of "stormy," Jimmy Groves bid farewell to "his friends and all" rather than "all of his friends," a few verb tenses and pronouns were altered.

The commonplace folk performer, his audience and fellow performers do not strive for change: they interact in a system of frequent repetition, enforcement and reinforcement to prevent it. In a small frame bungalow in the Smokies in 1963 I observed a corollary of Walter Anderson's law of self correction[36] in action when a seventy-five year old farmer-riflesmith-banjo picker named Lee Wallins told a lengthy *Märchen*.[37] As soon as he was finished, his friends and family, who had comprised his quiet audience and who had heard the tale only from him, ran down the list of things he had forgotten—a brief episode, the precise wording of a couple of speeches—which he should then tell to make the tale complete. These he dutifully told. The folk performer has also willingly accepted criticism from without. The agents for standardization with which the forklorist has customarily dealt (the broadside press, for example) would have been ineffective were it not for the fact that many a folksinger wants—would accept as the art or pop singer accepts—a correct text; several times I have been asked to secure "the right words" for singers who fear their memories to be faulty. The commercial recordings of the twenties and thirties, which are still played, have done more than influence Southern Mountain music, they have offered acceptable standard texts and melodies—less efficient than the standard texts and melodies of the art musician because they continue to involve aural-oral channels—and have rendered the repetoires of contemporary Southern Appalachian singers largely predictable.

The norm for the European—American folk performer is repetition. Whether he is an old man not known to his community as a singer, like Claude Proffit, a seventy-seven year old farmer whose small repertoire consists mainly of ballads learned from his parents and sung unaccompanied in a highly ornamented style,[38] or whether he is a young man who enjoys considerable local prestige as a musician, like Red Parham whose immense repertoire comes mainly from recordings, who wears a cowboy hat, sings like Lester Flatt and plays a guitar given him by the local Chamber of Commerce,[39] the folksinger repeats the songs he sings pretty much as he learned them. It is this repetitive nature of European—American folk production that makes the best singer in the old communities the man who can sing all night and never repeat[40] rather than the man who knows a few unusual songs. It is this which assists in the preservation of the textual complexity of European-American oral literature, and it is this which makes the historic-geographic comparative studies of folk types—songs or stories, barns or boats—feasible. If the usual singer were as creative as Dorrance Weir it would not be possible to recognize Barbara Allen or Lord Thomas after they had wandered about for four centuries. From the position of simple logic, the surprising thing is not how much variation there is within European-American folk tradition, but how little.

Within the repetitive norm there is perpetual small change.[41] Sources are misunderstood and the resultant error is repeated or semi-consciously rationalized: Ruby Bowman Plemmons insisted that Barbara Allen was buried in a "kire"—pronounced to rhyme perfectly with "higher"—and, though she did not know what that was, she knew it could not be a choir, for that is a group of singers in a church;[42] Claude Proffit has Georgie Allen say, "I want to die with the engine I love before I'm forty-three," when his source surely ran "...with the engine I love, number one hundred and forty-three."[43] Change also comes from forgetfulness, and probably the greatest single cause for the variation revealed by the comparative studies of the items preserved in academic folklore collections is the fact that old people have obligingly tried to recall forgotten tales or songs, which have long since ceased to function, for tenacious, friendly collectors. Linked with imperfect memory is minor innovation during performance: singers insert or omit unimportant words at the beginnings of lines, change verb tenses, names, pronouns and modifiers, but the average singer is no more likely to restructure a song completely than the average reader is to rewrite chapters of a novel. This small degree of permissable improvisation is very different from that which exists within an improvisational norm. Such a tradition, in which performance and composition are blended, the elements of the composition being drawn anew from a conventional stock at each performance, has been excitingly described as it exists among the singers of epics in Yugoslavia by Albert Lord.[44] While this is a kind of tradition quite different from that usual in the West, of which ballad singing is a neat example, improvisational performance may have European-American parallels. An example is provided by the keens composed by old women paid to lament at wakes in nineteenth century Ireland and possibly in the Pennsylvania coal fields.[45] The songs were similar in form, there were standard shreds and patches to use in composition and a moaning chorus during which to compose, but the keens had to relate to the corpse in question so that some extemporizing was inescapable.[46]

The breaking of the restrictive repetitive norm in a logical manner is creation.[47] The conscious production of the recognizably new within traditional European-American cultures is broadly distinct from the improvisations of the guslar or keener in that it is designed to issue stable things to be repeated by the performer-creator and others. Western creation is, then, an adjunct to—a regular and essential reaction to, product of, and source for—the repetitive norm; it is an antagonistic part of the same great tradition, bearing a relation to the repetitive norm similar to that borne by hippie to upper middle class values. The product of the person who utilizes some folk elements during the act of creation can be slight or great in its deviation from pre-existing, recognizable, acceptable wholes. As the deviation increases, the possibility of rejection by the audience increases as does the measure of the creator's venturesome spirit. The highly creative person is not fulfilling the traditional European-American expectation; like his product he is deviant. There are safe creations—folk the moment they are created—like the tune "Darlin' Sugar Lump" which North Carolina banjo picker Wes Sharp's father "made himself," most of which is "Sourwood Mountain" and the rest of which sounds like several other traditional tunes,[48] or the stanza which Ollie Ward, who lives about seventy miles up the Blue Ridge from Sharp, added to "Mole in the Ground."[49] As he learned the song from "the old people" it began with this stanza:

> Well, I wish I was a mole in the ground, ground,
> ground, ground, ground.
> And I wish I was a mole in the ground.
> If I's a mole in the ground,
> I'd root those mountains down, down, down,
> And I wish I was a mole in the ground.

His stanza, which he felt was just as good as the others in the song, was:

> And, I wish I was a pig on the bridge, goink,
> goink, goink.
> And, I wish I was a pig on the bridge.
> If I's a pig on the bridge,
> I'd dance just a little jig, jig, jig,
> And, I wish I was a pig on the bridge.

"Take That Night Train to Selma" is not a safe creation (nothing very like it can be found in the repertoires of Dorrance or other singers in his area), as such it is like the exhibition by the Eight American Painters at the MacBeth Gallery in 1908 or Joyce's *Ulysses*. It would be preposterous to compare Dorrance's abilities with those of Glackens or Joyce, but given his circumstances (a "disadvantaged" upbringing in a rural setting where the lone acceptable art of men—the only thing a man could do primarily as the fulfillment of an aesthetic urge—

was to make music, where the dominant ideas differed in some respects, such as the regard for education and progress, from those flowing in the American mainstream) his artistic courage—or cultural deviation—is comparable. In attempting to understand creation by people partially bound by folk practice, I have fallen back on my comparativist training and noted two factors which pop up with some regularity in the biographies of European-American artists of tradition who have, like Dorrance or the other men described in this book, made new things. One of these deals with the sources employed during creation, the other with the relation of the creator to his group.

The contemporary performer whose culture includes strong folk components can choose for performance from among a variety of models ranging from those which were archaic when he was first exposed to them as a child, to those which were the latest ideas of our society when they were presented to him on television yesterday. The norm is to accept a whole from tradition or from outside. Safe creation generally consists of innovation within a single model or combination of similar models coming from the same source. The adventurous creator frequently combines models selected from different cultural inventories: a simple example is Hobart Smith playing old tunes banjo style on the piano;[50] a more complicated one is Bill Monroe meshing white and black, urban and rural, sacred and secular elements in the development of bluegrass music.[51]

The sources for the elements present in any performance of "Take That Night Train to Selma" by Dorrance Weir are diverse. Pop Weir could ignore the annual visits of Uncle Dave Macon and the recordings of Jimmie Rodgers and the Carter family, but the hillbilly music which was popular in rural New York while Dorrance was learning his music gave him much of his style. The Southern mucicians, Dorrance said, had more leisure time than their Yankee counterparts and were, therefore, more creative; the first Southern music he heard was very exciting. He feels that he plays and sings in a Southern style which has been out of style for thirty years; after listening to himself on tape, he remarked that he could have "made a million" recording in the thirties. He accompanies all of his songs with a guitar played with a flat pick. That guitar is a big Harmony which set him back fifteen

dollars; it has a pair of holes in the front from which he extracted
some electrical apparatus to give to Ken Kane (amplified guitars, he
says, are not part of his style), and a larger and less regular hole in
the back, the result of a cigarette-caused fire which took place in the
bed of his pick-up truck, "Old Green." The guitar has been used to
"back up" the violin, piano, or accordion at square dances in central
New York since about 1880. The guitarist in the dance band was also
the dance caller. It was but a short step from there to the guitar's use
in accompanying songs, and several men of Pop Weir's generation do
use the guitar for song accompaniment, but they do not use picks and
they employ simpler chordal patterns and fewer "runs" than Dorrance
does. Dorrance's Depression era Country accompaniment not only has
antecedents in the generation of musicians which preceded him, but
also modern support in the generation which follows him: in the spring
of 1965, Dorrance led a band he had named "The Slim Pickin's"
and composed of his brother, Tad, on the fiddle and friend, Clyde Olson,
on bones and harmonica, at the high school his sons attended; there,
despite facetious prodding by the others in the band at a bar before
the performance, he did not sing "Take That Night Train to Selma";
there he picked up the name "hootenanny" for a musical gathering
and noticed that many young people play the guitar and sing, though
in a manner quite different from his. While he says he sings like a
Southerner, calls several of his songs "rebel moaners" and (especially
if he has had a little too much to drink) may even attempt a Southern
accent, his singing voice is only moderately nasalized, is not pitched
above his speaking voice, and he uses almost none of the exaggerated
phrasing of the Country recording artist. His naturally pitched, even,
slow singing style is less like that on the usual hillbilly recording than
it is like that of his father, Ken Kane, or Jesse Wells, a man in his seventies
who knew Pop Weir and considered him and his sons "geniuses," who
called dances at house parties as a young man and who sings to simple
guitar accompaniment. To Jesse Wells I devoted a good deal of time[52]
(and a good gallon of sweat haying in) because he seemed to exemplify
the older tradition in Dorrance's area and was, therefore, useful in
understanding Dorrance's sources. Like his father and Jesse Wells,
when Dorrance has finished a song he stops playing and singing abruptly.

This stylistic characteristic is conceivably related to the Northeastern practice of speaking rather than singing the last word or words of a song,[53] which was done also in Ireland.[54] At the least it is quite different from the Southern practice of ornamenting or retarding the song's last line or following it with conventionalized instrumental punctuation, such as playing the melody through or tacking on "shave and a hair cut—two bits."

The work situation in Rochester brought to Dorrance's mind "Night Train to Memphis," a Country song which appeared during the Second World War, was featured in a motion picutre in 1946, recorded recently as both an instrumental and a vocal, and heard occasionally on the radio in upstate New York in the winter of 1964-1965.[55] The melody of "Night Train to Memphis" carried that song's form into Dorrance's song, but its content inspired only one line: "Take that night train to Selma." The "Memphis" tune was not used without change; it became inextricably tangled with "Gimme That Old Time Religion." "The Old Time Religion" has been frequently printed[56] and it remains in the Country music repertoire.[57] Its tune has been separated from its text and reused.[58] Dorrance associated the song with the other hillbilly numbers in his repertoire and sang it frequently, often inserting the names of people present for Paul and Silas: "It was good for Hank and Haunchy and it's good enough for you." When Harriet Ottenheimer transcribed the tune of "Take That Night Train to Selma," she noted, "the melody of the last verse strangely sounds quite a bit like 'Gimme That Old Time Religion.' A curious correspondence."[59] Said Dorrance of his melody:

> The tune is not original in any way, I don't believe. I think it's something like "Gimme That Old Time Religion" or "Take That Night Train to Memphis" or something like that. It's just—just fits it, that's all.[60]

"Gimme That Old Time Religion" not only affected the melody, it provided the form for the fouth stanza he composed.

The ideas in Dorrance's song were drawn from his prejudices.

Central New York is no haven for liberals. It was an area infested with Copperheads during the Civil War as their descendents do not mind admitting, and a series of prejudices thrive there today. The old-time central New Yorker does not share in the defensive prejudice of the citizen of Deep South whose fear results in rationalizations (the Negro has "a double skull" or no morals): he is, rather, like the Southern Mountaineer, the owner of a little store who told me in December, 1962, that as far as he was concerned Negroes were equal to him, better than him if they had an education, but that did not mean that he wanted any Negroes to settle in his mountains. A gentle, seventy-four year old woman, who knew Pop Weir, once said, "I don't know why, I just don't want any niggers around here."[61] With this attitude, Dorrance was raised. There has never been any movement of Negroes (or Italians) into Dorrance's hills.[62] But, newspapers, radio and television carry an awareness of flux on the outside to people far from the areas involved; an old man living far back in the mountains of central Pennsylvania, in contrasting the good old days with the bad new ones, in June of 1966, spoke for many country people when he listed "nigger marches" along with the bomb and the Russians as the great threats of the modern world. The mass media alone may not formalize such sentiment into a Rural Power movement, nor may they be potent enough to cue "Take That Night Train to Selma," but they constantly remind the person, no matter how isolated, that the old order is giving way. They kept Dorrance and his audience abreast of external events, reinforcing their ripe prejudices, and providing him with material (stanzas 17, 20-26). Dorrance has also worked in the cities in the vanguard of rural prejudice and in competition with non Anglos. There a fearful, rationalized prejudice was added to his tough, if less specific and active, traditional prejudice. A part of this urban bred rationalization oozing into the countryside through channels like Dorrance's song is the link between the Negro and Italian. Dorrance asks where all the slaves of ancient Rome went, implying that the Italian is part Negro: the identification of the Negro and Italian (both are dark, foreign) has parallels in the recent urban fad of ethnic slur riddles.[63]

    Expressions of prejudice as song are not rare. The neo-Nazis have issued recordings: "Ship Those Niggers Back," poorly performed in Country and Western style and copyrighted by G. L. Rockwell, comes in a jacket which pictures Martin Luther King, Negroes, and a monkey in a boat.[64] The Ku Klux Klan released recordings on the "Fiery Cross" label, some of which parodied hymns.[65] Dorrance's song suggests sending black people back to Africa (stanza 8) and incorporates parts of "Gimme That Old Time Religion," but he did not know of these recordings. Comic Ethiopian songs were as popular in central New York during the last half of the nineteenth century as they were elsewhere in the North. Among the more plentiful hymnals and Grange song books stacked in piano benches and second hand stores in Dorrance's area, are still to be found a few cheap little books containing grotesque woodcuts and songs like "I'se Gettin' Up a Watermelon Party," "Dar's a Rooster Roostin' on de Roost," and "De New York Nigger."[66] Jesse Wells sang one called "I'se One of the Family Now" which he learned from his mother who got it in turn off a piece of sheet music which had a "great picture" of an "autocratic coon" dancing in striped pants on the cover. Dorrance sings songs from that era, but not in that vein. He has, however, heard songs like Jesse Wells', which deals with the stereotype of the Negro as shiftless— "I won't peel potatoes or I won't split wood"—exactly the idea which engendered the plan to send the lazy Italian to Selma where he would feel at home with lazy Negroes. These songs could have helped Dorrance in the development of a humorous song derogatory to the Negro; they certainly did not serve to diminish his prejudices any.

"Take That Night Train to Selma" did not begin as an anti-Negro topical song (that was, by and large, his audience's idea); it began as a satirical song designed to "give the needle" to an individual. Dorrance had used song in this fashion before. He often sings "The Year of Jubilo," a song written by a man with an Abolitionist heritage,[67] known by Jesse Wells, and common in the older tradition of New York State.[68] He learned it from a record in about 1931[69] and sings it because of the first line, "O say now, darky, have you seen the master with the moustache on the face." He does this to tease good naturedly a fiddler friend of his who sports a large moustache.

A song which is frequently requested at parties is one that he composed as a tight parody of the pop song "Leave the Dishes in the

Sink, Ma" which came out at the end of World War Two:[70]

> Leave the dishes in the sink, Aub;
> O, leave the dishes in the sink.
> Each dirty plate will have to wait,
> Tonight we're goin' to celebrate,
> Leave the dishes in the sink.
>
> Leave the fishes in the Lake, Clyde;
> O, leave the fishes in the Lake.
> Each dirty trout will have to pout,
> Tonight we're goin' to do without,
> Leave the fishes in the Lake.[71]

He made the song up when he was living at a construction camp near Binghamton, New York. Its purpose was to chide Aubrey Dawes, whose job it was to wash the dishes (a duty he rarely performed), and Clyde Olson, the most avid of many avid fishermen on Otsego Lake, who preferred fishing to cleaning up. Both of them often left Dorrance, the cook, to tidy the shanty; he retaliated with a song.

Dorrance describes the only other song he has ever composed:

> I used to sing about this fella I worked with in Rome, and he **goosed his mother-in-law** one night, an' she turned around and, oh, she slapped him. And, I thought an' thought an' thought, and I thought, how can I make something rhyme with that? And now [strums the guitar and sings to the tune of "Frankie and Johnny"]:
>> Artie, o, he got drunk,
>> Drunker than he ever saw.
>> O, Artie he got drunk
>> And he goosed his mother-in-law.
>
> [he stops, laughing] All at once it came, you know. And he used to crack his car up every weekend and I'd make up songs about him hittin' telephone poles.

> We stopped at this little local gin mill. And the old
> fellow would bring out this guitar an' we'd sing for
> awhile. We had a ball. . . . I had a song about a
> mile long about poor old Art Sears. Yes I did. It's
> gone. He got in three wrecks in one day. He hit a
> fence post and a telephone pole and a mail box and I
> had it all in. Three different verses about him.[72]

Songs composed like Dorrance's to satirize an individual were known in Britain, in the mine patches and, especially, in the lumber camps.[73] Newfoundland villages have singer-composers who use song to criticize those who deviate from established modes of behavior.[74] Dorrance's songs all exactly parallel these satirical songs in intent and mood, and a scholar presented with the bare texts might include them in the British American satirical song tradition. However, Dorrance seems not to have learned his technique, but rather, to have combined natural penchants for satire and song into a personal little polygenetic tradition of satirical song.

The musical sources of "Take That Night Train to Selma" are to be found in the old tradition of central New York (c. 1870- present) and in recorded Country music (1923-present). The Country music which Dorrance and his friends like is not totally unlike the old New York tradition (both share in the regularity of Anglo-American folk music) and, while its texts and tunes are not those of the old tradition, it has been inserted into the same slot in the culture: it functions in the same manner providing dance music for young people, entertainment for their elders, an aesthetic outlet for the manly male, and a means to local prestige. The old tradition, itself far removed—degenerated, advanced—from singing ancient ballads unaccompanied, is about dead, except insofar as it survives as strong influences in Country music. But, the tradition of playing and enjoying home-made music is most alive. In creating his song, Dorrance also utilized extra-musical elements: ideas drawn from attitudes and experiences, both traditional and personal, and from socialized and idiosyncratic abilities—from, for examples, living in the country, laboring periodically in the city, watching television, fighting in the Second World War, speaking

English, and making connections between things not obviously connected.

In composing "Take That Night Train to Selma," then, Dorrance provides us with an example of the adventurous creator selecting from among a broad range of models. The second characteristic of the European–American creator of tradition which struck me in looking through such biographical information as we have is that he is an unusual person: often his behavior is out of alignment with the strictest delineation of the traditional role of his sex in his society. This is evidenced in his relations with the opposite sex (he is often a bachelor when it is the norm to be parent and spouse), or his economic situation (he is often a failure at his chosen occupation, changing jobs frequently when it is the norm to be a steady provider).

One full study of a European–American folk creator is there to see: Edward D. Ives' biography of Larry Gorman (1846-1917), a poet of the Northeastern lumber woods. Gorman, the author of numerous satirical songs, never held a skilled job, though he worked as a "sort of useless fellow" at many unskilled ones around the lumber mills, brick yards and railroad beds, in the woods and ditches, at fishing and farming. He was considered odd, a loner; not popular among the men, he liked children, dressed as a dandy on Sundays, and enjoyed gossiping with the women.[75] At about the time that Gorman married at the age of forty-five, Anthony Piotrowski, his wife and daughter, arrived in Pennsylvania's anthracite area. Like many other Poles, Piotrowski sought a new life in the mines around Wilkes-Barre; he was a small man, however, mining was too much for him and most of his life was spent picking slate and bony in the screen room—a boy's job. He composed a series of poems in Polish: three were published, apparently at his own expense, in a flimsy, eight page booklet, *Oryginalne Śpiewki Górnicze;* more were set to traditional Polish melodies and sung in the saloons he frequented. The poems were bitter descriptions of miners spilled to their deaths from a cage, burned by gas, or drinking away their meagre pay—of immigrants bilked, mocked, and depressed in an alien land. Surviving photographs show that Piotrowski dressed well and that at different times he had a full beard or flowing moustache. He served as librarian for the small collection of a Nanticoke Polish society and passed his love of books on to his only daughter. The memory of him is vague but consistent: he was a thoughtful man who kept to himself, neither well known nor liked by the men who were making it in the New World's coal mines.[76]

Piotrowski is reminiscent of Gorman as is Aaron Mountz, a gentle, impractical south-central Pennsylvania wood carver who never married and whose unsuccessful attempts at bridge construction, well digging, and farming led him as an old man to a mental hospital.[77] Others have revealed their social individualism in other ways. Ola Belle Reed is a frank, politically savvy woman who composed (at a time when her health was poor) a ballad out of a legend she learned from her uncle, and a song which described her life and hard times: "Born on the mountain fifty years ago...too many mouths to feed...barefoot in the summer and on into the fall...I've endured, I've endured, how long must a man endure?" The Depression drove Mrs. Reed, her mother and twelve brothers and sisters from the mountains of North Carolina to the hills at the eastern end of Mason and Dixon's line. To support her family, she has worked as a maid, a salesgirl, a member of several bands which played Southern music on low watt radio stations, at auctions and parks in Maryland and Pennsylvania, and as the co-manager of a large country store.[78] Considering her Blue Ridge raising, her successful performance in public roles is as unusual as Anthony Piotrowski picking slate and collecting scrip with the boys, or Larry Gorman gossiping with the women. Ollie Ward, who invented a banjo style by blending bluegrass and old-time thumbing techniques in addition to creating the stanza of "Mole in the Ground" quoted above, similar new stanzas for "The Little Brown Jug," and over twenty Country and Western style love songs, is a bachelor like the men who compose songs of social censure in Newfoundland [79] and the Pennsylvania German artist Lewis Miller.[80] Ward, a genuine woman hater (had my wife not taken a walk during the recording session, it would have been a failure), was well liked by the men in his area. His big frame house, located a goodly distance from any kind of road, was a place to which his married neighbors liked to retreat for a long, rough night of liquor and music.

The balance of the story is told by a man like Jesse Wells who has traveled little, whose family has lived in the Toddsville area for five generations, who has lived all his life in a house his grandfather bought in 1851, and who has worked the same 140 acre farm, been married to the same woman, and a member of the same Grange hall for better than half a century. In the thirty-three different songs he put on tape, the variation between the renditions of some of the longer songs was considerable; as recording continued his texts filled out and evened up. This was because the only singing he had done since his courting days consisted of absent minded snatches during milking. Only once has he consciously altered a song; it is significant that the change was to only one half of one line in the song "The Old Arm Chair,"[81] that the change was made five decades ago, but that he remembers clearly doing it.

The proposition that creativity is often a trait of the individual who is imperfectly adjusted to the traditional European-American society can be set up for viewing on a broader if shakier base by a consideration of groups in which the artistic norm is different from that in the traditional European-American society. These groups are either not European-American or not societies. The Afro-American norm is not repetitive; a Negro blues cannot be tracked through time and space with the facility that an Anglo-American ballad can be. The Afro-American norm tends toward and beyond the improvisational and a successful study of Afro-American traditions often must involve a concern with parts rather than wholes—motifs rather than types.[82] I had the pleasure of studying daily a small self-identified group of black boys in Philadelphia for eight disconnected months in 1966 and 1967; their active oral reportoire encompassed a range from neat repetition of quatrains, to improvisation with traditional components, to free wheeling creation out of experience and environment within thin traditional frames. Not only is Afro-American folk expression unlike European-American (the material may be the same but the treatment is not), but also, of course, the traditional society is structured differently. There may be a link between the fact that the norm in black folk art is improvisational and the fact that the black folk social system is matrifocal—mother is the steady provider, father is footloose and cool, a subject for hate and imitation.[83] To chase this idea into the woods: the computer has cautiously revealed a correlation between those African societies with matrilineal kin groups and those with highly developed art.[84]

The European-American groups within which creation among artists of tradition is so common as to be normative are composed of men alone; ballad hunters in the lumberwoods encountered song makers as well as singers,[85] and one of the few American material expressions which is continually labeled "folk art" and chances to be, actually, both folk and art is the scrimshaw developed by the whalemen on long, tedious voyages.[86] The male group often brings carriers of different cultures together, including some with a working knowledge of nonfolk aesthetics, men like Jack Thorp, son of a wealthy New York lawyer, international wanderer, cowboy and author of "Little Joe, the Wrangler" (Laws B5),[87] or D. J. O'Malley, also son of a New Yorker, cowboy and poet, the author of "When the Work is Done Next Fall" (Laws B3).[88] The art that the group produces out of the variety of available models is generally bound to the group's new, shared experiences; prisoners, for example, tell jokes about convict homosexuality and mean wardens.[89]

Creativity and the all-male group seem to become interdependent: the group needs the creativity to produce a repertoire with which it can collectively identify, and the creativity needs the group and its characteristics for source material. Lou Sesher, a man in his seventies who has spent a life on riverboats mainly in the Ohio Valley, has in his seemingly unfathomable memory a great number of tall tales. These deal with a multitude of subjects, but his creativity, which is displayed in his paintings, his boat model building, and the one tall tale he has invented, is deeply involved with the river. His own folktale was made up recently and comprised the second page of a letter dated December 14, 1967; *punctatim et literarum* that page follows:[90]

> I noticed a write up about a whale on a boat,
> this I recall, I was maybe 8 yrs old at Dayton
> K'y [between the lines he notes, with an arrow to
> this spot, "true to here"] So I built the story
> up from there, as they did not know what happened
> to it. Here it is, Last known exibit was Sistersville
> W. va, the boat was on stopped at Ravens Rock,
> W. va. and I heard that a very large cat came on
> the boat, ate the whale, could not get out the

> door, so they continued on to P.g'h showing a large stuffed cat. when the cat purred the viborations of the boat sent large ripples all the way across the river. I know two men that knows this to be true but, if called on, they would take 5th amendment, and I would not blame them Wish you-all a Merry Christmas.
>
> Lou

The esoteric content of the traditional art of the male group separates it from that usual to agricultural societies. The sailor sings, "A is for the anchor,"[91] the lumberjack, "A is the axe,"[92] the aviator, "A is for the Air Force boys,"[93] but, while farm children might recite "A is for apple" to learn the alphabet, it would be hard to imagine a song popular among farm wives beginning "A is for apron" and continuing with a dictionary of kitchen accoutrements. The esoteric nature of the creations of the male group seems to reflect a fascination with an often very new, often temporary way of life and an awareness that it is different from the life which was known to the group's members when they were boys—the life which remains normal outside of the group and which turns about a responsible man accompanied by his wife and children.

The relevance of the coincidence in individuals of creativity and social individualism to Dorrance Weir is real, though not dramatic. To begin: "Take That Night Train to Selma" and all of the other songs he has composed originated while he was living away from his family in construction camps with only men around him.[94]

Dorrance has a fine family: a charming wife and two popular, athletic sons of whom he is proud. With great difficulty he is paying the way of his older son through an expensive New England college, and he provides both of them with large wardrobes—all in the spirit of the American cliche of presenting the offspring with the comforts the parents never had. There lies Dorrance's frustration—an economic frustration which causes him to drink, to nurture prejudices, and to seek ambiguously friends who have more education and money than he has.

Rural central New York in the late nineteenth century was rich. Cash from dairy products and hops—among the most profitable of which were grown in Dorrance's county, Otsego[95] brought boxy big Victorian Houses, enormous basement barns and hop kilns to the landscape, jigsaw trim and turrets to the older buildings, and popular culture, with its Sunday picnics, gadgetry, and coon songs, to the farm people. But with the initial two decades of our century came the blue mould to kill the hops and the full impact of the competition from the West, where the land was flat and fertile and modern agricultural machinery was practical.[96] Hop growing went to the West Coast;[97] much of the profitable turn-of-the-century dairying[98] followed the mid-nineteenth century cash crop, wheat,[99] to the Middle West; the New York farmer was left suddenly poor. Otsego County suffers today from out-migration; its population is old.[100] It is spotted with abandoned farms and farms which only appear to be abandoned; it is one of the poorest counties in New York, despite the jolly wealth of a few of its villages.[101] In these surroundings Dorrance grew up: in poverty with an insistent memory of prosperity. No topic of conversation in the taprooms and parlors of today is more popular than the happiness of the hop picking era.

The poverty of Dorrance's childhood contrasted visibly with the life of the tycoons and middle class in nearby Cooperstown and with the prosperous memory. For those who have remained on the farm—"Never Mortgage the Farm" and "Stay on the Farm, Boys" are in Jesse Wells' repertoire—the warm memory assists in their determination to stick it out, but Dorrance's father frequently moved trying different jobs, attempting to gain economic stability. When they did settle at the "home place" in Oaksville, Pop Weir and the boys worked as garbage men— a fact Dorrance never mentions. Eventually Pop opened a tiny country store sided with brick imprinted asbestos and tin advertisements. His store, situated across the highway from the Oaksville Hotel, was a great place for political discussions and music making, if not for spending money.

After the war Dorrance worked for several years as a shoemaker, but the business failed; a friend of his commented, "Dorrance was a good cobbler but a lousy businessman." Some of his brothers were carpenters, so he took up that trade. A story told with amusement by people who do not know him as well as by those who do, recounts how Dorrance signed on his first job as an experienced carpenter when he did not even know how to shingle a barn. But he taught himself to be a competent wood worker, a cabinet maker and a specialist in building concrete forms. He followed this construction work to many cities, to Binghamton, Rome, Utica, and Rochester. The work paid well, though never as well as the jobs some of his friends had, but it was irregular with long lean stretches about which he bitterly complained. During part of the period of his song's development he was out of work, first because the winter makes construction jobs hard to find, and later, because, much against his will, his union put him home on strike. He got some work building forms at a college a bit more than twenty miles from his home and at a bridge near Toddsville. His dissatisfaction with his work while he was adding to "Take That Night Train to Selma" prompted him to buy some hill land, some hogs and calves. He worked clearing the land, building fences, caring for his stock, and cultivating a large garden. In 1965, he talked of building a home on his new ground, of becoming a self-sufficient farmer; his enthusiasm resulted in healthy heifers and a bountiful garden. In 1966, he stood at the corner of his field, tossed seeds in all directions and never lifted a hoe against the weeds the land he had cleared began to be reclaimed by the forest; his stock was sold; and he talked of a new scheme. He still wanted to quit construction work, but not to be a farmer; he and some friends were planning to go to the Catskills to cut the good timber left standing on the steep slopes. The work was as dangerous as it was profitable and his wife talked him out of the plan.   Again he followed construction work, living with the men in the camps, living through periods of feast (though never as large a feast as he would wish) and famine. In 1968, according to his father-in-law, he was laid off or had gone off on strike and had secured a job working on the new school being constructed on the outskirts of Cooperstown. He sold his house and took an apartment in Fly Creek while building a new home in the hills where his garden had been. He planned to stay on there after the school had been constructed, vacuuming the floors and driving the bus; the pay was poor—a cut above what the government considers the level of poverty, a cut below what it considers comfortable—but it was steady and the trouble with construction work, he said, was that "when you make money, you really make it, but when you don't make it, you don't make nothin'."

If there is a causal connection between creativity and an unusual socio-economic situation, that connection would be worth a psychologist's attention.[102] It would seem most logical that creativity and social individuality are parallel results of a genetic or childhood tendency toward oblique behavior. There are cases, however, in which creativity and individualism apparently influenced each other directly.[103] Larry Gorman seems to have been a slipshod worker partially because of his poetic preoccupation, and he may have been driven to wandering by the satirical songs he composed.[104] The opposite direction of influence seems to be the stronger. It was not until his wife died and his children were adopted that Gib Morgan began wandering from oil field to oil field, making up tales.[105] Paul Mc Clintock is a burly, mustachioed construction worker from central Pennsylvania, whose father was a singer, and who has been a hillbilly music fan all his life; his talk is punctuated with quotations from Country songs and he remembers crying all night when the radio brought the news that Uncle Dave Macon was dead. He never composed a song until his wife left him and he was given thirty days for nonsupport. Incarcerated among men, he made up some "dirty stories," a song about the judge who sentenced him (a song which netted him an additional sixty days), a song about the jail, a sentimental one about his native hills, and a religious song. That was twenty years ago; he still sings the songs on occasion but he has composed no new ones since his brief stay in jail.[105] Tab Ward, a successful North Carolina mountain farmer in his early sixties, spent much time playing the banjo and fiddle as a youth. During the long years of his marriage his talent lay fallow, but as soon as his wife died he built a banjo and began singing again. He was encouraged by his friends who considered him "a good hand on the banjo,"[106] and he was stimulated by an unchallenged competition with Frank Proffitt, a neighbor who made it big with the folk festival crowd,[107] a thing which mumbly, off-beat Tab Ward could not do. But he became a creator, decorating his banjo with geometric ball point pen designs, altering old songs and making up new ones. His grandson taught him the text of Child ballad number 286 out of a book[108] (Tab cannot read); he accepted the text with minor, largely grammatical, changes, but he completely rebuilt the refrain and made a tune for it out of tradition's whole cloth. He changed the color of the eyes that shine like diamonds in the song "Little Maggie,"[109] which he said he learned from a G. B. Grayson record, from blue to brown because his late wife's eyes were brown. And he used material from tradition and experience to compose a song, "Batching on the Farm,"[110] about the hectic life he has led since his wife's death.[111]

The notion that there is a causal relation between creativity and unconventional socio-economic behavior is supported by the fact that the creation is often concerned with the individualistic situation—perhaps exactly that which freed the creator so that he could create or drove him to creation: Tab Ward's song composed after his wife's death dealt with her death and his new life; Anthony Piotrowski who failed as a coal miner, wrote poetry about the hardships of miners. Dorrance's song and its development were squeezed out of his economic frustrations. In the cities he had to work shoulder to shoulder with people he was raised to believe were not his equals. His song had its inception in just such a work context and it continued to be directed against those who were in economic competition with him. Dissatisfied, Dorrance sought friends—sought cautiously with fear of rejection—at higher economic levels than his own. He found that they were amused by his song and partially to please them, and partially to please his wife who shared and molded his desires, he kept working at it, retaining the stanzas they liked, rejecting those they did not.

Dorrance saw a connection between his music and his economics. His family, he felt, was musical because they did not have money enough to buy a radio or phonograph and, therefore, had to produce their own entertainment. He saw his music as a means toward economic gain, much as his father used his fiddling. Most of the transcriptions from tape given above reinforce that idea as do those which follow. Once after singing "Take That Night Train to Selma" he paused and thoughtfully said:

> Do you know though, Hank, If I put my

> mind to it I really think I could make a song
> that would sell on this integration. And keep
> it good, and still on the edge.[112]

He would like his song to bring him money. Because he knows it will not, he says he does not work at song making:

> There's no doubt that several more verses could
> be made to this ["Night Train to Selma"], but
> I never devoted any time to it.[113]

> I've made up a few verses to "Frankie and
> Johnny"[114]—never recorded them in any
> way— and few songs that I could go with—for
> what?[115]

He kept working on "Take That Night Train to Selma," however, because it gave him a way to attack some of those who were preventing him from achieving the stability he wanted (thereby consoling himself for its absence) and because, while it brought him no money, it did bring him a degree of prestige among people who had the money he did not have, the money which has kept him uneasy, sensitive, fluctuating from depression to joy—a creative person.

Creativity is frequently a byproduct of the collision of cultures. This is most obvious in border country; for example, where the great Tidewater and Mid-Atlantic folk cultural regions run side by side through east-central Maryland from north of the Chesapeake to the Potomac west of Washington, a variety of syncretistic folk buildings stand as frozen creativity. In a world of television and cheap print, cultural frontiers are mental rather than geographic. Among the unrelated mentalities which form this frontier in America are those of the individualistic creators in traditionally oriented communities. It may be that no situation could be less likely to foster creativity than one involving non-cooperative capitalism with little profit possible, fundamentalist morality with its modesty and guilt, and authoritarian patrifocality with its strict roles for men, women, and children—all of which are characteristic of the culture shared by the members of the conservative European-American community. The art in these communities—and it is no less art than that of more innovative or progressive communities—is one of tight refinement, of repetition; the singing is solo and constrictive and conceivably related to the stringent morality which pervades such communities.[116] Yet, in this restrictive matrix there are people who manipulate their culture, who shatter the repetitive pattern and produce new things. These creators may have been freed to do so by an elimination of their customary responsibilities (as in the case of sudden bachelor Tab Ward) or have been forced to do so because of a dissatisfaction with their own culture brought about by a comparative knowledge of other cultures (as in the case of our friend Dorrance Weir).

IV

Who will study the song composed by Pop Weir's son? Not the folklorist, for he studies songs which have texts printed in books written by folklorists. He might collect and archive it because it does live in the repertoire of a singer who knows songs which have passed from mouth to ear to mouth for awhile,[117] but rendering it and its creator full attention is another matter.

A serious consideration of an expression of culture must involve an analysis of more than the obvious whole: components and contexts must also be taken into account. Some brand new songs are novel recombinations of folk elements and are true folksongs at the instant of their creation. "Take That Night Train to Selma" is no folksong; it includes, however, components which are folk—the prejudice which is its foundation,[118] aspects of the way in which it is sung—and to deny its folk parts would be as myopic as considering it folksong. A song not folk at birth, we are told, must "enter oral tradition" to achieve the modifier "folk." Dorrance's song has not entered tradition and probably never will; yet, the audiences for which it was performed liked and constantly requested it, and the local musicians learned the tune so that they could accompany its singer-composer. Entering tradition is a form of acceptance; in a real sense "Take That Night Train to Selma" was accepted, though less actively than "Leave the Dishes in the Sink, Aub," which some of his friends sing, and considerably less actively than B. N. Hanby's "Nellie Gray" which Dorrance attributed to Stephen Foster or Carson J. Robison's "Wreck of the Number Nine" which Dorrance and many others sing without associating it with Robison.[119] "Take That Night Train to Selma" can provide the folklorist with some ideas as to how one[120] (passively) acceptable, (partially) folk song was made. To wait until it enters tradition would be to miss the opportunity of observing a song under construction.[121]

The folklorist is accustomed to recognizing the easily recognized polar ends of art. The overview which ignores the nuances of things partially folk and the fact of folk creativity is the natural result of the text-thing concern of the collector.[122] The collector must work in an environment where the same conservatism supports attractive things like the singing of old ballads and unattractive things like racial prejudice and a hatred of education.[123] Too often when he encounters the bearers of tradition he is like the Haitian urban romantic[124] who loved the country but resented the existence of the peasants in the countryside: wondering how such degenerate people could know such beautiful folklore items, the collector snatches the texts he was looking for and retreats to civilization before getting to know the people; in the safety of his study he can assign numbers to the text and the text to a name in a headnote and to Redfieldian puppets in a skimpy introduction.

The failure of the folklorist in studying only the parts of culture he wants to study has its parallels in other disciplines. The anthropologist has developed the concepts necessary for a study of American culture—Goodenough's ideas on culture, for example[125]—yet he persists in escaping to exotic cultural islands to return with fascinating data on people relatively easy to understand. The scholars in the chronological disciplines—American studies, art history, English literature, U.S. history, and so on—maintain an interest mainly in the great and the obvious. There is no time during their evolutionary pogo-sticking from one meaningful event to the next—William and Mary to Queen Anne to Chippendale to Hepplewhite and Sheraton—for a consideration of the strong, at times quantitatively dominant, conservative fibers in the Western fabric. Studies of selected areas of oral retention, of preliterate cultures, of the progressive mainstream leave vast areas of American life unexplored. Some of these areas are hard to travel, some are staggeringly repulsive, but until they are studied our generalizations about both America and culture and the programs based on those generalizations can be correct and workable only by accident.

NOTES

ACKNOWLEDGEMENT: Harriet Ottenheimer of the Anthropology Department, Tulane University, transcribed the tunes. My wife, who shares my fondness for the Weirs, typed the manuscript. Professor Kenneth S. Goldstein read a preliminary report on this project in 1965. I am very grateful to all three of them for their assistance.

[1] The information on Pop Weir comes not only from his children, friends and acquaintances, but also from a poor tape recording made by Don O'Brien in about 1961. Entitled "Weir's Music," it represents forty tunes in two distinct sessions played and sung by Pop, Dorrance, Tad, and Buster Weir.

[2] Tape-recording, July 9, 1965.

[3] Laws J8. G. Malcolm Laws, *American Balladry from British Broadsides* (Philadelphia, 1957), p. 132, gives reference to Michigan and Kentucky versions, and to two broadsides and a songster. Edith Fowke, "British Ballads in Ontario," *Midwest Folklore*, XIII:3 (Fall, 1963), pp. 133-162, reports some Canadian versions. Irish texts can be found in Colm O'Lochlainn, *Irish Street Ballads* (New York 1960), pp. 2-3, and James N. Nealy, *The Second Book of Irish Ballads* (Cork, 1964), pp. 77-79.

[4] This was written by Benjamin Hapgood Burt, and published in 1907; see Sigmund Spaeth, *Read 'Em and Weep* (Garden City, 1926), pp. 255-257; Ira W. Ford, *Traditional Music of America* (Hartboro, 1965), pp. 273-276; Charles O'Brien Kennedy, *A Treasury of American Ballads* (New York, 1954), pp. 338-340. Pop Weir's tune was about the same as Spaeth's (which was omitted along with the text from the paperback edition of New York, 1959); his text had been much "improved" by tradition.

[5] This song about a man who plans to sell his pasture to the railroad, buy "a high silk hat and a gold top walking cane, and a watch you can twist right around your wrist that don't need any chain," and return after hobnobbing with the aristocrats to his mountain shack, is a favorite of Dorrance's. He considers it a "Weir family song" unknown to anyone else; it does, indeed, seem rare. The New York State singer of ballads, Sarah Cleveland, who has composed sentimental Country style songs on the Vietnam mess, recognized it as a song sung by the older people in her family when I asked her about it at Kenneth Goldstein's house in Philadelphia, December 21, 1966. It was recorded between 1924 and 1933 by Frank Crumit as "A High Silk Hat and a Walking Cane"; see John Edwards, "Old Time Singers No. 1 Frank Crumit," *Country & Western Spotlight*, Special Edition (1962), p. 8.

[6] Laws G26. G. Malcolm Laws, *Native American Balladry* (Philadelphia, 1964), p. 225. More references and versions can be found in Jan Philip Schinhan, *The Frank C. Brown Collection of North Carolina Folklore*, IV (Durham, 1957),

pp. 357-358, and *Colorado Folksong Bulletin,* II (1963), p. 40. There seem to be five versions in the Library of Congress; see *Check-List of Recorded Songs in the English Language in the Archive of American Folk Song to July, 1940* (Washington, 1942), pp. 282, 298, 302, 447; all are Southern. It is apparently surprising that this song of commercial hillbilly origin and dissemination would have been sanctified by Laws; Edith Fowke, for example, omitted the Laws number from "The Wreck of Number 9" in *Traditional Singers and Songs from Ontario* (Hatboro, 1965), p. 59. G26 was not listed with the other Laws ballads on hillbilly records in footnote 13 of D. K. Wilgus' "An Introduction to the Study of Hillbilly Music," *Journal of American Folklore,* 78:309 (July-Sept., 1965), only because he used the first edition of *Native American Balladry* for his study.

[7]This song was written and recorded by Stuart Hamblen and was a best selling record in 1949; see Nat Shapiro, *Popular Music,* II (New York 1965), p. 287.

[8]Dorrance's version amounts to a detailed description of venereal disease and is a good deal dirtier than the version in E. R. Linton, *The Dirty Song Book* (Los Angeles, 1965), pp. 46-47.

[9]Sung square dance calls like those used by Pop Weir, Dorrance and others in the area, such as Jesse Wells who will be introduced later in the paper, can be found in Norman Cazden, *Dances from Woodland* (Ann Arbor, 1955); for examples, Dorrance's call for "Marching Through Georgia" and Jesse Wells' call for "Captain Jinks" are similar to those given in Cazden's collection from the Catskills. The singing call, usual at square dances in Pennsylvania, New York and New England, seems to have become common about 1870; see S. Foster Damon, *The History of Square Dancing* (Barre, Mass., 1957), p. 39.

[10]This party took place on August 7, 1966. I made several recordings at parties and on August 9 of the same year recorded an uninterrupted hour of a party. Individual songs were not altered for the tape recorder, nor was the chancy order of performance changed for recording, but Dorrance had some integrity about the songs he wished to put on tape, and this list, which I wrote down from memory immediately after the party, is more representative of his functioning repertoire than any of the tapes I have or have heard.

[11]I heard "Take That Night Train to Selma" with regularity between March and August 1965 in the Oaksville-Cooperstown-Whig Corners area. When I noted any changes in the text, I wrote them down and arranged for a recording session as soon as possible. Unless stated otherwise all quotations from the song came from tape recordings made on June 17 (2), July 9, 1965, January 5, August 9, 1966 and September 11, 1968; or from one long text dictated on July 9, 1965. I have also transcribed texts from two recordings (one made in October and one later in the fall of 1965) by Minor Wine Thomas, Jr., of Cooperstown, and one made in the first week of July, 1966 (3) by Marilyn Kimball of Oxford, Ohio. I am deep in debt to Mr. Thomas and Miss Kimball for their recordings.

[12] Tape recording, July 9, 1965.

[13] Tape recording, January 5, 1966.

[14] Tape recording, January 5, 1966.

[15] Tape recording, January 5, 1966.

[16] Tape recording, August 9, 1966.

[17] Information from Per E. Guldbeck of Cooperstown, November 26, 1965.

[18] Cottages like Kane's and Jesse Wells' are mentioned in Talbot Hamlin, *Greek Revival Architecture in America* (New York, 1964), p. 266. They are lineal descendents of the Yankee Cape Cod, for which see Ernest Allen Connally, "The Cape Cod House: an Introductory Study," *Journal of the Society of Architectural Historians*, XIX:2 (May, 1960), pp. 47-56.

[19] Cf. Archer Taylor, *Proverbial Comparisons and Similes from California* (Berkeley and Los Angeles, 1954), p. 25.

[20] "Marching Through Georgia" was written by H.C. Work during the Civil War. It has been frequently printed: Harry Dichter and Elliot Shapiro, *Early American Sheet Music: Its Lure and Its Lore, 1768-1889* (New York, 1941), p. 116; *The Scottish Students' Songbook* (London, c. 1900), p. 300; *Heart Songs Dear to the American People* (Boston, 1909), pp. 310-311; *Songs That Never Grow Old* (London, New York, and Toronto, 1913), p. 57; Thaddeus Gorecki, *Song Book: Central High School of Philadelphia* (Philadelphia, 1925), pp. 14-15; Edward Arthur Dolph, *Sound Off* (New York, 1929), pp. 353-355. It is a common dance tune in New York; see footnote 9 and Lettie Osborn, "Fiddle-Tunes from Orange County, New York," *New York Folklore Quarterly*, VIII:3 (1952) p. 214; Herbert Haufrecht and Norman Cazden, "Music of the Catskills," *New York Folklore Quarterly*, IV:1 (1949), p. 44.

[21] This song was written by Dick Reynolds and Jack Rhodes; it was a best selling record in 1963; see Nat Shapiro, *Popular Music*, I (New York, 1964), p. 188.

[22] "Willow Tree"—"Bury Me Beneath the Willow"—is very popular in Dorrance's area; a distinct local variant of the tune has developed. Normally Dorrance does not remember the name of the artist who made the recordings from which he learned the songs; he thinks, however, that he learned this from a Carter Family record. The Carters recorded it in 1927; their rendition was issued on the Victor, Bluebird, Montgomery Ward, and Regal Zonophone labels; see John Edwards, "The Carter Family: A Discography," *The Sunny Side Sentinel*, 2:3 (April-October, 1963), p. 4. The song is very common in the South; for references:

58   FOLKSONGS AND THEIR MAKERS

Henry M. Belden and Arthur Palmer Hudson, *The Frank C. Brown Collection of North Carolina Folklore,* III (Durham, 1952), pp. 314-317; Jan Philip Schinhan, *Brown Collection,* V (Durham, 1962), pp. 189-190; *Colorado Folksong Bulletin,* II (1963), pp. 16-17.

[23] Transcribed from a tape recording made on July 9, 1965. Questions about a song's provenance would have been out of place that night, but at a longer, typically folkloristic tape session on July 14, 1965, Ken Kane said that he learned the song from his father who was not much of a singer, and that his father's version was "nine miles long." His father did not yodel, though he did sing a nonsense refrain. The song may have a Gaelic origin. It was printed commonly in Ireland, has been found in lumberjack tradition and may have been worked over in the West to produce "Get Along Little Dogies"; see Alan Lomax, *The Folk Songs of North America* (Garden City, 1962), pp. 357-358, 372-375; and the notes by Diane Hamilton to *The Lark in the Morning* (Tradition, TLP 1004), which includes an Irish version of the song, "Rockin' the Cradle," on Side A, Band 4. For American Texts: MacEdward Leach, *Folk Ballads and Songs of the Lower Labrador Coast* (Ottawa, 1965), p. 286; Lester A. Hubbard, *Ballads and Songs from Utah* (Salt Lake City, 1961), pp. 232-233; Vance Randolph, *Ozark Folksongs,* III (Columbia, 1949), pp. 117-119.

[24] Tape recording, July 9, 1965. He momentarily forgot the standard form of stanza eight (the seventh stanza in this rendition) and recomposed it slightly while he was singing.

[25] This song was rewritten out of a traditional song by the late Paul Clayton. As sung by Billy Grammer, it became a best selling record in 1958; see Shapiro, *Popular Music,* I, p. 238. Clayton's source is listed in Arthur Kyle Davis, *Folk-Songs of Virginia* (Durham, 1949), p. 315. I collected a traditional pre-Clayton version called "High Sheriff" from Wesley Sharp, South Turkey Creek, Buncombe County, North Carolina (June 8, 1963; August 1, 1964).

[26] "The Prisoner's Song" on the flip side of "The Wreck of the Old 97" sold more than seven million copies after its issue in 1924; see Archie Green, "Hillbilly Music: Source and Symbol," *Journal of American Folklore,* 78:309 (July-September, 1965), pp. 217-218. Both songs are commonly sung today throughout rural America; for "The Prisoner's Song": Belden and Hudson, *Brown Collection,* III, pp. 411-416. Dorrance said he had heard Ken Kane's parody before and did not think it was particularly funny; it began, "If I had the wings of an angel and the balls of a hairy baboon. . . ."

[27] Transcribed from a tape recording supplied by Minor Wine Thomas, Jr. Note that in this difficult circumstance Dorrance relied on the original three stanzas—the ones he liked best. Note, too, that he announced it as a song dealing with Negroes, not Italians, despite its content.

[28] Cf. John Greenway, *American Folksongs of Protest* (New York, 1960), p. 85.

[29] Ben Shahn, *The Shape of Content* (New York, 1960), pp. 39-40.

[30] Frederick L. Gwynn and Joseph L. Blotner, eds., *Faulkner in the University: Class Conferences at the University of Virginia* (New York, 1965), p. 229.

[31] Edward D. Ives, *Larry Gorman: The Man Who Made the Songs* (Bloomington, 1964), pp. xiii-xv, 129.

[32] For example see the essays by Phillips Barry and Charles Seeger in MacEdward Leach and Tristram P. Coffin, eds., *The Critics and the Ballad* (Carbondale, 1961).

[33] Recorded in Washington by Paul Clayton Worthington and myself, May 14, 16, 1962.

[34] (Chapel Hill, 1960), pp. 77-78, 104-106, 124-127, 172-175, 185-187.

[35] This is put into academic context by Kenneth S. Goldstein, "Bowdlerization and Expurgation: Academic and Folk," *Journal of American Folklore*, 80:318 (October-December, 1967), pp. 381-382.

[36] See Walter Anderson, *Kaiser and Abt* (Helsinki, 1923), pp. 397-403.

[37] Recorded north of Marshall, Madison County, North Carolina, June 10, 1963. In my text-happy stupidity, I published the tale without the commentary in *Tennessee Folklore Society Bulletin*, XXX:3 (September, 1964), pp. 92-97.

[38] Recording and interview, Todd, Ashe County, North Carolina, June 12, 1963.

[39] Recordings and interviews Asheville, August 6, 1961; South Turkey Creek, June 8, 1963; Weaverville, June 16, 1963; all are in Buncombe County, North Carolina.

[40] Cf. W. Roy MacKenzie, *The Quest of the Ballad* (Princeton, 1919) p. 229.

[41] See Stith Thompson, *The Folktale* (New York, 1946), p. 436; Tristram P. Coffin, *The British Traditional Ballad in North America* (Philadelphia, 1963), pp. 1-8.

[42] Our comparison of Mrs. Plemmons' new and old texts also revealed that the transcriber of the texts—of all people the one who would least want to

make a change in a text—had made an error in 16 of 276 lines. With a recording to refer to, he had done just slightly better than Mrs. Plemmons' memory.

[43] His text can be found in *Mountain Life and Work*, XL: 4 (Winter, 1964), pp. 26-27. The song, Laws G3, is best seen in John Harrington Cox, *Folk-Songs of the South* (Hatboro, 1963), pp. 221-230.

[44] Albert B. Lord, *The Singer of Tales* (New York, 1965), part 1.

[45] George G. Korson, *Minstrels of the Mine Patch* (Hatboro, 1964), pp. 149-150.

[46] For keening see T. Crofton Croker, *Researches in the South of Ireland, Illustrative of the Scenery, Architectural Remains, and the Manners and Superstitions of the Peasantry* (London, 1824), pp. 172-181; Leith Ritchie, *Ireland Picturesque and Romantic* (London, 1837), pp. 208-209; Mr. and Mrs. S. C. Hall, *Ireland: Its Scenery, Character & c.*, I (London, 1841), pp. 223-229; Kathleen A. Browne, "The Ancient Dialect of the Baronies of Forth and Bargy, County Wexford," *The Journal of the Royal Society of Antiquaries of Ireland*, LVII (1927), p. 130; Kevin Danaher, *In Ireland Long Ago* (Cork, 1964), pp. 174-175.

[47] To relate this to H. G. Barnett's important *Innovation: The Basis of Cultural Change* (New York, 1953), all creativity is innovation, though not all innovation is creativity, for he includes accidental novelties as innovations (for examples, pp. 208-212, 233), and I feel that a creation is a conscious change; its origin can be an accident, of course, so long as that accident is considered and consciously retained or refined. The qualitative division in creativity with regard to the newness of the product and the uncertainty of its acceptance, which seems useful to me in understanding relationships within and around folk cultures, is not something he worries particularly about; still it is akin to his notion of compatibility (safe creation is compatible, adventurous creation may or may not be compatible) discussed in chapters XII and XIII, and his statement that the advocate of novelty can thereby jeopardize his prestige (pp. 318-321). In the terms of a different system, adventurous creation results in prime objects, repetition and safe creation in replication; see George Kubler, *The Shape of Time: Remarks on the History of Things* (New Haven and London, 1962).

[48] Recordings and interviews, South Turkey Creek, Buncombe County, North Carolina, June 7-9, 1963; August 1, 1964. For "Sourwood Mountain," one of Sharp's favorite tunes, see Schinhan, *Brown Collection*, V, pp. 162-166, (the B tune is like that embedded in "Darlin' Sugar Lump").

[49] Recording and interview, near Beech Creek, Watauga County, North Carolina, August 5, 1964. For "Mole in the Ground": Belden and Hudson, *Brown Collection*, III, pp. 215-216; Schinhan, *Brown Collection*, V, pp. 124-126.

[50] Recording and interviews, Saltville, Smyth County, Virginia, August 30-31, 1962. For further examples, hear Harold Courlander, *Folk Music U.S.A.*

"TAKE THAT NIGHT TRAIN TO SELMA"   61

1(Folkways, 4530), side C, band 15; Alan Lomax, *Banjo Songs, Ballads and Reels from the Southern Mountains* (Prestige International, 25004), side B, band 8.

[51] Ralph Rinzler, "Bill Monroe--'The Daddy of Blue Glass Music'," *Sing Out!*, 13:1 (February-March, 1963), pp. 5-8. His ideas were intensified in a paper, "A Dynamic Approach to Tradition—Bill Monroe," read at the American Folklore Society Annual Meeting, Boston, November 20, 1966.

[52] Recordings and interviews, near Toddsville, Otsego County, New York, November 17, 23, December 21, 1964; January 11, March 27, May 23, July 1, 1965; August 12, 1966.

[53] For the declamando ending see Phillips Barry, *The Maine Woods Songster* (Cambridge, Mass., 1939), p. 6; Horace P. Beck, *The Folklore of Maine* (Philadelphia and New York, 1957), p. 90; Edward D. Ives, "Twenty-One Folksongs from Prince Edward Island," *Northeast Folklore*, v, (1963), pp. 13, 63; Bruno Nettl in Leach, *Labrador*. p. 17.

[54] Eric Cross, *The Tailor and Ansty* (New York, 1964), p. 28.

[55] Between May, 1942, and August, 1965, eight records of "Night Train to Memphis" by Roy Acuff were issued on the Columbia, Okeh, Capitol, and Hickory Labels. Acuff also sang the song in the Republic film "Night Train to Memphis" copyrighted April 18, 1946. See Elizabeth Schlappi, *Roy Acuff and his Smoky Mountain Boys* (Denton, Md., 1966), pp. 15, 22-23, 26, 32. *Popular Recordaid* (Philadelphia, 1965) lists two instrumentals and three vocals by Del Wood, Duane Eddy, Grandpa Jones, Don Cornell, and Roy Acuff. John B. Frankhouser, station manager of WNOW, Town and Country Radio, York, Penn., writes (November 30, 1967) that it also appeared on the Anita Kerr Singers' album *Nashville Sound*.

[56] G. D. Pike, *The Jubilee Singers and Their Campaign for Twenty Thousand Dollars* (Boston, 1873), p. 198; J. B. T. Marsh, *The Story of the Jubilee Singers; With Their Songs* (Boston, 1880), p. 158; Daniel B. Towner and Charles M. Alexander, *Revival Hymns* (Chicago, 1905), no. 9; *Songs of Faith* (Nashville, 1933), no. 295. It is common in both black and white tradition in the South: Belden and Hudson, *Brown Collection*, III, p. 674; Schinhan, *Brown Collection*, V, pp. 297-298; John W. Work, *American Negro Songs and Spirituals* (New York, 1940), p. 99; R. Emmet Kennedy, *More Mellows* (New York, 1931), p. 15.

[57] The manager for Jim and Jesse and the Virginia Boys writes on the back of their album, *The Old Country Church* (Epic LN 24107), "no matter how big or small the crowd, there are always requests for *The Old Time Religion.* . . ."

[58] In *Spiritual Folk-Songs of Early America* (New York, 1964), p. 218, George Pullen Jackson notes that the same tune, associated with a text of "Sinner Man," appears in Cecil J. Sharp, *English Folk-Songs from the Southern Appalachians*,

II (London, 1932), p. 291. Another example: Don Yoder, *Pennsylvania Spirituals* (Lancaster, 1961), pp. 280-281.

[59] Letter dated July 22, 1966.

[60] Tape recording, July 9, 1965.

[61] This woman's home is described in "The Wedderspoon Farm," *New York Folklore Quarterly*, XXII:3 (September, 1966), pp. 165-187. That article provides a little folklife background for Dorrance Weir and his songs. These books give information on culture in the general area during the early nineteenth century: Elizabeth L. Blunt, *When Folks Was Folks* (New York, 1910), a pretty good book patterned after E. H. Arr's *New England Bygones* (Philadelphia, 1880); Jared van Wagenen, Jr., *The Golden Age of Homespun* (New York, 1963), a somewhat slaphappy book which generalizes about the frontier from an imperfect knowledge of upstate New York; and Louis C. Jones, ed., *Growing Up in the Cooper Country: Boyhood Recollections of the New York Frontier* (Syracuse, 1965). The area described in Emelyn Elizabeth Gardner, *Folklore from the Schoharie Hills, New York* (Ann Arbor, 1937) is nearby but presents a culture different from Dorrance's; farther away but more relevant is the area described in Anne Gertrude Sneller, *A Vanished World* (Syracuse, 1964).

[62] W. A. Anderson, *The Population Characteristics of New York State* (Ithaca, 1947), pp. 13-15, shows that of the thirteen areas of the State, that in which Dorrance lives has the fewest Negroes and the fewest foreign born people.

[63] See Donald C. Simmons, "Anti-Italian-American Riddles in New England," *Journal of American Folklore,* 79:313 (July-September, 1966), pp. 475-578.

[64] "Ship Those Niggers Back" "We is Non-Violent Niggers," Odis Cochran and guitar with "the 3 Bigots," Hatenanny Records, H-1, G. L. Rockwell, 1964, 45rpm record.

[65] Marcello Truzzi, "Folksongs on the Right," *Sing Out!,* 13:4 (October-November, 1963), pp. 51, 53.

[66] These titles were taken from two books found near Dorrance's home: *Christy's Panorama Songster* (New York, n.d., c. 1860) and *Hamlin's Wizard Oil Song Book* (Chicago, n.d., c. 1899).

[67] "Kingdom Coming" or "The Year of Jubilo" was composed by Henry Clay Work (1832-1884). It was written and first published in the midst of an intensive advertising campaign in 1862, and was printed frequently from that time on. See Dichter and Shapiro, *Sheet Music*, p. 116; Edwin Wolf 2nd, *American Song Sheets, Slip Ballads and Poetical Broadsides, 1850-1870. A Catalogue of the Collection of the Library Company of Philadelphia* (Philadelphia, 1963), p. 82 (lists 13 sheets); Minnie Earl Sears, *Song Index Supplement* (New York, 1934),

p. 167 (4 references); David Ewen, *Songs of America: A Cavalcade of Popular Songs* (Chicago, 1947), pp. 109-111; Sigmund Spaeth, *Weep Some More, My Lady* (Garden City, 1927), pp. 114-115; Willard A. and Porter W. Heaps, *The Singing Sixties* (Norman, 1960), pp. 268-270; Irwin Silber, *Songs of the Civil War* (New York, 1960), pp. 306, 317-319. Some of those printings were George F. Root, *The Bugle-Call* (Chicago, 1863), pp. 54-55 (on the back cover it is noted that 30,000 sheets of "Kingdom Coming" have been printed and that the song is "sung wherever our flag floats"); *Scottish Students*, pp. 302-303; *Heart Songs*, pp. 152-153; Dolph, *Sound Off*, pp. 353-355. It was in the Hutchinsons' repertoire: Carol Brink, *Harps in the Wind* (New York, 1947), p. 296. For collected texts: Belden and Hudson, *Brown Collection*, II, pp. 541-543; Schinhan, *Brown Collection*, IV, pp. 275-276; *Colorado Folksong Bulletin*, I:3 (November, 1962), p. 15. The tune has been used for dancing; for example: Frederick Knorr and Lloyd Shaw, *Cowboy Dance Tunes* (Caldwell, 1949), p. 14; and it is on this cheap record which was for sale in a Cooperstown supermarket in 1965: Roy Horton and His String Band, *Square Dances* (Grand Prix Series, KS-128), side B, band 5.

[68] Harold W. Thompson, *Body, Boots and Britches* (New York, 1962), p. 278.

[69] Ben Gray Lumpkin, *Folksongs on Records: Issue Three* (Boulder and Denver, 1950), p. 16, item 116 is a Victor recording "The Year of Jubelo" by Frank Crumit (see footnote 5).

[70] Having listened to Dorrance's parody, I was surprised to find that this song did not have a Country and Western origin; indeed, it was copyrighted on February 21, 1945, by Spike Jones, Milton Berle and Gene Doyle: see *Library of Congress Copyright Office Catalog of Copyright Entries*, Part 3, vol. 40, Part 1, no. 3 (1945), p. 320, no. 10346.

[71] Tape recording, June 17, 1965.

[72] Tape recording, August 9, 1966.

[73] Ives, *Gorman*, chapter 11.

[74] John Szwed, *Private Cultures and Public Imagery: Interpersonal Relations in a Newfoundland Peasant Society* (St. John's, 1966), pp. 97-98.

[75] Ives, *Gorman*, pp. 64, 81-84, 112, 126, 132-137, 183-185.

[76] Information on Piotrowski comes from letters from Marie Kocyan of Wilkes-Barre, Pennsylvania, May 9, September 25, October 24, 1967; and taped interviews with Mrs. Kocyan May 24, 1967, and with Mrs. Kocyan, Mrs. Vincent Znaniecki, Mrs. Leon Lentz, and Mrs. Joseph Pluto on August 31, 1967.

[77] Milton E. Flower, "Aaron Mountz, Primitive Woodcarver," *Antiques,* LXXVII: 6 (June, 1960), pp. 586-587; the same scholar's *Wilhelm Schimmel and Aaron Mountz: Wood Carvers* (Williamsburg, 1965), pp. 13-15.

[78] Recordings and interviews Oxford, Chester County, Pennsylvania, January 23, February 6, 20, April 3, 17, 19, 21, November 27, 1966; March 9, April 12, 24, June 1, October 19, December 10, 1967.

[79] See John Szwed's excellent paper in this volume.

[80] Donald A. Shelley in Robert P. Turner, ed., *Lewis Miller: Sketches and Chronicles. The Reflections of a Nineteenth Century Pennsylvania German Folk Artist* (New York, 1966), p. xviii. Miller cannot be considered a folk artist, although his art does reflect some stylistic influence from fraktur. He is used here because so little is available on genuine American folk artists, like the anonymous ladies who cultivate flowerbeds in the sandy front yards of the southern Tidewater. Neither is there much information available on folk craftsmen- producers of objects primarily practical and secondarily aesthetic in function. The folk craftsmen I have known have produced things of great strength and beauty, but they have not been adventurous creators; some craftsmen, however, are highly innovative, such as Chester Cornett, a Kentucky chairmaker who is being intensively studied by Michael Owen Jones: see his "A Traditional Chairmaker at Work," *Mountain Life and Work,* XLIII:1 (Spring 1967), pp. 10-13.

[81] Two "Old Arm Chairs" are common in tradition; this is the one found in Gale Huntington, "Folksongs from Martha's Vineyard," *Northeast Folklore,* VIII (1966), pp. 72-75, 82.

[82] Cf. Daniel J. Crowley, *I Could Talk Old-Story Good: Creativity in Bahamian Folklore* (Berkeley and Los Angeles, 1966).

[83] The roles of men and women in Afro-American society have been linked with traditional artistic expression before; see Charles Keil, *Urban Blues* (Chicago, 1966), pp. 20-28, 147-156; Roger D. Abrahams, *Deep Down in the Jungle: Negro Narrative Folklore from the Streets of Philadelphia* (Hatboro, 1964), pp. 7, 21-39; Paul Oliver, *Blues Fell This Morning* (New York, 1960), pp. 93-117.

[84] Alvin W. Wolfe, "The Complimentarity of Statistics and Feeling in the Study of Art," in June Helm, ed., *Essays on the Verbal and Visual Arts* (Seattle, 1967), pp. 149-159.

[85] Roland Palmer Gray, *Songs and Ballads of the Maine Lumberjacks* (Cambridge, Mass., 1925), pp. xvi-xx; Franz Rickaby, *Ballads and Songs of the Shanty—Boy* (Cambridge, Mass. 1926), pp. xxvi-xxviii.

[86] See Marius Barbeau, "All Hands Aboard Scrimshawing," *The American Neptune,* XII:2 (April, 1952), pp. 99-122; Walter K. Earle, *Scrimshaw: Folk Art*

of the Whalers (Cold Spring Harbor, N.Y., 1957); Edouard A. Stackpole, *Scrimshaw at Mystic Seaport* (Mystic, 1958).

[87] Austin E. and Alta S. Fife, eds., *Songs of the Cowboys by N. Howard ("Jack") Thorp* (New York, 1966), especially pp. 5-7, 28-37.

[88] John I. White, "A Montana Cowboy Poet," *Journal of American Folklore* 80:316 (April-June, 1967), pp. 113-129.

[89] Bruce Jackson, "Prison Folklore," *Journal of American Folklore* 78:310 (October-December, 1965), pp. 317-329.

[90] David A. Walton has carefully collected a great body of material from Lou Sesher. Walton's collection was published in *Keystone Folklore Quarterly*: XI:4; XII:1; XII:3: XII:4; XIII:1. I recorded an interview with Lou at his home in North Charleroi (Lock Four), Pennsylvania, August 25, 1967, corresponded with him regularly from 1967 to 1970, and had access to ten tapes made in 1966 and 1967, which Dave Walton donated to the Ethnic Culture Survey of The Pennsylvania Historical and Museum Commission, Harrisburg, where copies of my field notes are also deposited. The towns mentioned in Lou's tale are on the Ohio River. Its central incident is related to the ancient and broadly distributed Winnie the Pooh motif K 1022.1 (Wolf overeats in the cellar [smoke house] cannot escape through the entrance hole); see Stith Thompson, *Motif-Index of Folk-Literature*, 4 (Bloomington, 1957).

[91] Kenneth Peacock, *Songs of the Newfoundland Outports*, III (Ottawa, 1965), pp. 885-886. In volume 1 on pp. 125-126 Peacock gives a fisherman's alphabet, a parody by Chris Cobb, who is the author of several satirical songs and on whom Peacock provides frustratingly scanty information in his "The Native Songs of Newfoundland,"*National Museum of Canada Bulletin 190, Contributions to Anthropology*, 1960, part II (1963), p. 219.Before presenting his text of "The Sailor's Alphabet," in *Chanteying Aboard American Ships* (Barre, Mass., 1962), pp. 52-54, Frederick Pease Harlow mentions an unprintable "vulgar" version. I obtained a crumpled manuscript, entitled *ALPHABET*, beginning "A Is for Ass," and continuing obscenely on, from a twenty-eight year old Negro state employee in Harrisburg, Pennsylvania, January 10, 1968. It is like the alphabet songs not only because of its rhythm and rhyme scheme and the facts that it circulates among males and provides in-group glosses for the letters of the alphabet, but also because its tone is self-conscious; it remarks cutely under U: ". . .gee it must be hell to hear language like this."

[92] Earl Clifton Beck, *Lore of the Lumber Camp* (University of Michigan Press, 1948), pp. 37-40; William Main Doerflinger, *Shantymen and Shantyboys* (New York, 1951), pp. 207-209.

[93] Leach, *Labrador*, pp. 178-179.

[94] It could be that the combination of a song tradition with an all male

situation often yields satirical songs—a possibility, reinforced by reality of Dorrance Weir, which may have implications for the historical connections which have been suggested between different Anglo-American satirical songs.

[95] "Hops—Otsego County, N.Y.," *The Northern Farmer*, II:10 (October, 1855), p. 457: "The Hop produce of Otsego County is now much larger than that of any County in the State or in the United States." See Marion Nicholl Rawson, *Of the Earth Earthy* (New York, 1937), pp. 129-141.

[96] The causes for agricultural decline in hilly New England described in Harold Fisher Wilson, *The Hill Country of Northern New England* (New York, 1936), chapters V-VII, are applicable also to hilly central New York.

[97] W. A. Anderson, *Social Change in Central New York Rural Community* (Ithaca, 1954), pp. 22-23.

[98] The fall of northern New York cheese making recounted in Loyal Durand, Jr., "The Historical and Economic Geography of Dairying in the North Country of New York State," *The Geographical Review*, 57:1 (January, 1967), pp. 24-47, has relevance for Dorrance's area where cheese making was a common home industry. After knowing me for a while Dorrance ventured a definition of folklore: "It's the way my mother made cheese."

[99] Ulysses Prentiss Hedrick, *A History of Agriculture in the State of New York* (New York, 1966), p. 332.

[100] Anderson, *Population Characteristics,* p. 43, shows that the area which includes Otsego County leads New York in the percentage of its population in the 55-64, 65-74, 75 and over brackets.

[101] *Basic Statistics for Counties of New York* (Albany, n.d., statistics as of 1956), shows that the per capita income of Otsego County is $1284, below the State average of $2163 and the Upstate average of $1773. It ranked 45th out of the fifty-seven counties for which per capita incomes were available—particularly surprising when it is realized that a large number of very wealthy people live in the County.

[102] I relegate any apology I might have for venturing into mental realms where I have no expertise to this footnote. Perhaps a psychologist should have done this study.

[103] On the other hand, George Edwards, a bachelor whose health was bad, who moved often, drank heavily, never held a responsible job, dressed like a dude when he had the money, and came from a song writing family, was not at all creative · see Marilyn Kimball, "George Edwards, Catskill Folksinger," unpublished M.A. Thesis, Cooperstown Program, State University College of New York at Oneonta (March, 1966).

[104] Ives, *Gorman,* pp. 49-50, 78, 126-128, 133.

"TAKE THAT NIGHT TRAIN TO SELMA" 67

[105] Mody C. Boatright, *Gib Morgan: Minstrel of the Oil Fields* (Dallas, 1965), especially pp. 26-27.

[106] Interview near Laurelton, Union County, Pennsylvania, March 16-17, 1967.

[107] Frank Proffitt got some money from "Tom Dooley," recorded two LP's (Folkways 2360, Folk Legacy FSA-1), and his death was followed by a number of obituaries: *Mountain Life and Work*, XLII:1 (Spring, 1966), p. 6; *Sing Out!*, 16:1 (February-March, 1966), pp. 22-24; *North Carolina Folklore*, XIV:2 (November 1966), pp. 12-20; *Tennessee Folklore Society Bulletin*, XXXII:1 (March, 1966), pp. 1-5.

[108] Richard Chase, *American Folk Tales and Songs* (New York, 1956), pp. 120-121. This paperback is available in several stores in Boone, the town nearest to Tab Ward's farm on the Watauga River.

[109] Excepting that adjective his song is the same as that performed by many Southern Mountain Banjo pickers; for example, Madison County, North Carolina, singer Obray Ramsey on Kenneth S. Goldstein, *Banjo Songs of the Southern Mountains*, (Riverside, RLP 12-610) side 1, band 1.

[110] This appears on *The Beech Mountain Ramblers*, (Mountain Craft Music, 101), side 2, band 5. Tab Ward felt that a recording would bring him wealth and fame, so he sank his life savings into this LP which was recorded by a local movie house operator and peddled by a neighbor along with "folk" toys to tourist shops. He used the same traditional tune and some of the same stanzas in an earlier composition for which see: *Mountain Life and Work*, XL:3 (Fall, 1964), pp. 59-60.

[111] Recordings and interviews, Sugar Grove, Watauga County, North Carolina, December 18, 1962, June 13-14, 1963, August 5, 1963.

[112] Tape recording, August 9, 1966.

[113] Tape recording, January 5, 1966.

[114] His Laws I3 is the Johnny Cash long legged guitar picker version recorded as "Frankie's Man Johnny," (Columbia 41371).

[115] Tape recording, July 9, 1965.

[116] The repetitive norm is logically consistent with a different attribute of European-American folk art: singing style as described by Alan Lomax; see his papers: "Folk Song Style," *American Anthropologist*, 61:6 (December. 1959), pp. 930-932; "Song Structure and Social Structure," *Ethnology*, 1:4 (October, 1962), pp. 439-441; "Special Features of the Sung Communication," in Helm, ed., *Essays on the Verbal and Visual Arts*, pp. 120-121; "The Good and the Beautiful in Folksong," *Journal of American Folklore*, 80:317 (July-September, 1967), pp. 214-218. The repetitive, innovative, or creative nature of a tradition can be revealed only by multiple recordings of the same item by the same performer;

analysis depends on careful ethnography and lends itself but poorly to computerization. Lomax with the computer and I with nothing but the usual guesswork have studied different aspects of the same tradition and arrived at compatible conclusions.

[117] Cf. Kenneth S. Goldstein, *A Guide for Field Workers in Folklore* (Hatboro, 1965), pp. 133-138.

[118] In an article on a black actress in *Look* (January 9, 1968), p. 72, it can be stated with confidence: "Nobody calls Diana 'nigger' anymore. The word has been swept out of style. . . ." Being publicly out of style and traditional are the characteristics a folk thing must have.

[119] Barnett in *Innovation*, pp. 386-389, distinguishes between active and passive acceptance. Entering oral tradition is an extreme form of active acceptance. On the inevitable continuum, Dorrance's song lies just to the passive side of the median.

[120] See Harold Benjamin, "Case Study in Folk-Song Making," *Tennessee Folklore Society Bulletin*, XIX:2 (June, 1953), pp. 27-30.

[121] For the difficulties inherent in getting at the origin of a song which has entered tradition, see Archie Green's fine piece of detective work, "The Death of Mother Jones," *Labor History*, 1:1 (Winter, 1960), pp. 68-80.

[122] Read chapter four of D. K. Wilgus, *Anglo-American Folksong Scholarship Since 1898* (New Brunswick, 1959), and especially pp. 336-343.

[123] Cf. Ralph Ellison, *Shadow and Act* (New York, 1966), pp. 38-41.

[124] Morin Dutilleul in Philippe Thoby-Marcelin and Pierre Marcelin's novel *The Beast of the Haitian Hills* (New York, 1964), especially pp. 12-14.

[125] Ward Hunt Goodenough, *Cooperation in Change* (New York, 1963), pp. 257-265.

A MAN AND HIS SONG:
JOE SCOTT AND "THE PLAIN GOLDEN BAND"

BY

EDWARD D. IVES

Lizzie Morse, the heroine of Joe Scott's "The Plain Golden Band." Photo taken at about the time of her second marriage in 1898.

A Man And His Song:
Joe Scott And "The Plain Golden Band"[1]

by

Edward D. Ives

The functional study of folksong has taken many different approaches to arrive at some understanding of what part songs play in the lives of the people who sing and listen to them. One very valuable approach has been through biography, and biography has as I see it four main places where it can shed light. First it can be used to study the *subjects* of folksong, and here one of the best examples is Américo Paredes' *With His Pistol in His Hand,* a study of the *corrido* of Gregorio Cortez and its hero.[2] Second it can be applied to the study of the individual singers in order to see the relations that exist between their lives and the songs they sang and learned. The best such study so far has been Ellen Stekert's dissertation, *Two Voices of Tradition,* an extremely careful examination of the repertoires and personalities of two singers.[3] Such studies may well turn out to be the most important, the most revealing of the ways folksongs really live and function, but as a corrective to conclusions drawn from such biographies I would suggest a third kind, the study of those who did not consider themselves singers but who were to varying degrees (some loved to listen, some got out of the room) the audience.[4] For my own part, I have chosen a fourth approach: the study of the *creator* of folksongs, the folk poet, and more specifically the woods poet: a woodsman or riverdriver who, working within a live and functioning tradition of song, created new ballads for the enjoyment of his fellow workers and which might be passed on by them in a predominantly oral tradition.

Not that we can or even should expect the folk to fit such neat distinctions. There will be overlapping, especially among the last three categories. A man may be an active singer of certain kinds of songs but part of the audience when it comes to other kinds. The creator of songs will probably also be a singer (I have found no exceptions yet), but at the very least he would have to be someone who had thoroughly internalized the tradition. Further than that, a man could be subject, singer and creator. Larry Gorman, for example, not only made up songs and sang them but through his songs he helped to create his own legend.[5] Enough of this. The distinctions are useful so long as we do not expect too much of them.

Then too, the word "creator" is a bit ambiguous, and I am just culture-bound enough to distinguish three levels.[6] First, we have the creativity of the individual performer brought to bear on a particular performance. In the strictest sense of the term any performance is a creative act since it brings into being something that wasn't there before, but I am more concerned with the conscious attempt of anyone recognized as a singer to make *this* particular performance something special. The proof of the presence of this level of creativity is in the considerable differences we find in performances by a single singer and in the singer's own statements (and the statements by his audience) that he sang a song well on some particular occasion but poorly on another.

A second level of creativity occurs when a singer makes changes in a particular song in order to make what he considers a better song out of it. I am thinking here of conscious changes, but I recognize that the line between conscious and unconscious is blurred and tenuous.

We all know singers who have repaired faulty rhymes, changed words, left out stanzas, added stanzas, or even changed tunes. Sometimes the changes are made at one swoop, but more often they are made with repeated singings, which certainly helps to blur the distinction between these first two levels of creativity. Yet they are different; the former works on the song only *as* it is sung, the latter normally occurs at some time *previous* to that singing.

Both of these levels of creativity operate on an already existing song, a "given," and the result is a unique performance or a unique variant. The third level of creativity, and the one I am especially interested in, occurs when an entirely new song is created. However much it may resemble other songs, it is still recognized by the folk as a *new* song, or, after it has become just one more "old song," it is still recognized as a song different from others. What is involved here is the more common definition of creation, I should say, like the birthing of a new poem. The best way to study this kind of creation would be to study living poets by talking to them about their art and by making a detailed study of their products. What do they write about? Just how do they go about it? What is the relationship between tradition and invention in their works? What relationship can we establish between the poet's personality and the products he turns out? And so on. It should go without saying that that is exactly what Henry Glassie and John Szwed have done in the other studies in this book.

A problem comes up here. In the study of folksong we are interested not only in what is created but also in what is accepted into folk tradition. Yet even this question of acceptance must be seen in its local context. If a local poet, a person so known, sends his work away to the city where it is published in magazines or books, he is of no particular interest to folklorists except that insofar as he is known in the community as a "real poet" he can help us understand what tenuous line there is between "real poetry" and "songs" in the mind of the folk. On the other hand, a man who makes up songs which he sings himself but which have not been collected from others will repay careful study many times over. Why, for example, were his songs rejected, or were they really "rejected" at all? It may be that they are thought of in the community as *his* songs, and it may even be that he doesn't want other people singing them, but if his songs are known *to* other people though not sung *by* them, they are still very much a part of local tradition. Dorrance Weir is an example of a man whose work has evidently never gone into oral tradition, yet the scholar who ignores such a man and sniffs at his productions as "not really folksongs" for this reason obviously does so at his peril.

Nevertheless, the question of acceptance and rejection is a real one, and it should be doubly interesting to be able to study people who made up songs that they not only hoped would be sung by their contemporaries but that actually were sung by them. But it takes a certain amount of time for a song to become so established, and given the moribund state of folksong tradition in the Northeast today, I don't think it is likely we will run into many people whose songs have become established in tradition who are still in fit condition to be talked to. We are caught, then, in a kind of double stretch: the closer a folk poet is to us in time, the more we can find out about him and the events he wrote about, but the further back we go the better chance we have to see what ballads get accepted into tradition and what changes that tradition may work on them.

The best solution would seem to be to look for a figure in the middle distance, the author of a group of ballads that have become thoroughly traditional yet whose career was recent enough so that we can still find out something about him and the events he chronicled. He would furnish us with a reference point to which we could relate distributional and historical studies of earlier ballads and more detailed biographical studies of recent folk poets. Such a man was Larry Gorman, except that he wrote satires and comical songs, not ballads. But eminently such a man was Joe Scott. His ballads are solidly in tradition, and there are both men and documents enough available to allow his story to be told. The full story--the complete biography and the detailed study of all his ballads-- will come, with God's good grace, in God's good time. What I will do here is first of all summarize his life and work; then I will give a sample study of just one of his ballads, "The Plain Golden Band."

I

Joseph William Scott was born in Lower Woodstock, New Brunswick, in 1867. Temperamentally unsuited to farming, he left home as a young man for the lumberwoods of Maine, arriving just as the burgeoning pulp and paper industry was creating a boom in the woods that would equal anything ever seen when lumber was king. He settled in Rumford Falls, a raw paper mill town and woods depot that had only been carved out of the wilderness a few years before Joe arrived, and he worked up and down the Androscoggin River, where he became known as a crack woodsman and river-driver and a great guy, a man among men--and among women. In 1894 he was jilted by a beautiful girl, Lizzie Morse, and it marked him. Except for a few side excursions which I'll mention later, he kept to the woods until that notoriously roaring life caught up with him and in 1916 he wound up in the Augusta State Hospital, where it took him almost two years to die of what his death certificate euphemistically called "general paralysis of the cerebral type."

Joe was not far different from thousands of other young provincemen who came to Maine to "cut the tall spruce down," but he left something behind: several ballads so much a part of Northeastern tradition that when I asked a man from Johnville, New Brunswick, if he knew any old songs, he said, "You mean songs like 'Benjamin Deane' and 'Howard Carey' and 'The Plain Golden Band'?", all three of them Joe's compositions (though my informant did not know this). No one, not even Larry Gorman, ever made a stronger impression on, or got more songs into the general tradition of Maine and the Maritimes than Joe Scott did.

Before I go on to a discussion of Joe Scott's ballads, someone should ask just exactly what are my criteria for saying a song was written by him at all. I've already had some things to say about such criteria in *Larry Gorman*,[7] but to begin with if I have a printed version with "By Joe Scott/ Price 10 cts" on it, I'll accept that as pretty compelling evidence that he was the author. Failing this, we can, with some caution, rely on ascription, especially ascription by someone who knew Joe or had bought songs from him. We can also check each ballad that has a verifiable historical basis against what we know of Joe's life to see if he had been in the right place at the right time to write that ballad. Finally, we have the evidence of style, the slenderest reed of all yet one that is far from useless (more about that latter). Of course, utter certainty is not possible in a study like this, but for most of the ballads I list as Scott's, any reservations I may have are probably no more than ingrained academic hedging on my part.

Let me give a couple of examples. The ballad "John Ladner" has been attributed to Joe by a couple of people who knew him, and there is nothing in the style of the piece that would gainsay his authorship.[8] In a general way, the place and date are right; John Ladner was killed on November 29, 1900, in Madison, Maine, only sixty miles from Rumford where Joe made his headquarters. But that sixty miles is across a height of land and Madison is on the Kennebec River, in an entirely different lumbering area, and while I have no evidence Joe was ever in Madison, I have very good documentary evidence that he was in the Rumford area that fall. Joe Scott almost certainly did not write "John Ladner." On the other hand, "Howard Carey"[9] is very generally ascribed to Joe, is like other pieces of his, and it is beyond reasonable doubt that he was around Rumford in the spring of 1897 when Howard Carrick hanged himself. I am perfectly sure that Joe wrote "Howard Carey." The evidence for authorship will be different for each ballad, but we can establish a pretty accurate canon.

I have appended a checklist of all of Scott's songs and ballads (including many doubtful items), with information on the number of versions I have found of each and their distribution. Quite obviously, five of these--"Benjamin Deane," "Guy Reed," "Howard Carey," "The Norway Bum," and "The Plain Golden Band,"–are the ones that won a real place in northeastern tradition. I should add that about 75% of all the texts I have are directly from oral tradition, the rest being from manuscripts people have sent me, newspaper and magazine reprints, and (in three cases) Scott's original slips. Now even a quick survey of the figures makes it clear that the entire tradition of these ballads was limited to New Hampshire, Maine, New Brunswick, Prince Edward Island, and Nova Scotia, which means that their distribution defines almost perfectly a folksong area which, while it is a part of general northern lumberwoods tradition, is still quite distinctly a subregion. There is a historical explanation for this region-within-a-region. Since before the Civil War, Maine woodsmen had been lured west by better wages, and the panic of 1873 only intensified their exodus, extending it into the late eighties. The vacuum in the Maine woods was filled by thousands upon thousands of provincemen who would work hard for the wages offered, and they kept on coming right up into the early years of this century.[10] But by the late nineties, when Joe Scott's ballads were going into tradition in Maine, the migration of Maine men to areas further west had pretty well stopped. Thus we find earlier songs like "The Jam on Gerry's Rock," (Laws C-1) or "The Banks of the Little Eau Pleine"[11] (Laws C-2) about equally distributed between the Northeast and the Midwest, but Joe's ballads came too late to have been transported to "the woods of Michigan," though in plenty of time to spread all over Maine and the Maritimes.

So much for the distribution of Joe's ballads. When we turn to their subject matter, we see that he worked with the same general themes that have attracted generations of writers in the broadside tradition: violent death, be it through murder, suicide, or accident; and love, always of course, disappointed or unhappy love. Two humorous pieces, "The Maid with the Golden Hair," and "Charming Little Girl," can be included under the second rubric, but they are funny and not pathetic, and pathos is the chord to which both of Joe's strings of love and death were tuned.

As for specific subjects, Joe almost always wrote about local events, yet all of his information was second-hand; I am quite certain that Joe was not an eyewitness to any of the calamities he wrote about (excepting, of course, "The Plain Golden Band," which tells his own love story). On the other hand, the people he wrote about were all people he could have known personally, and in fact he probably did know most of them. What he already knew of these people plus the details he could have picked up *via* the "bush telegraph" probably supplied him with most of his facts. He may have used newspaper accounts too, but the ballads show that he usually knew more about the events he chronicled than he ever could have gotten from the

newspaper accounts alone. Whatever his sources, we can say (as
many of my informants have said in praise of him) that he wrote
"about things that really did happen." The notable exception is
"The Norway Bum." There was no loss of life in Norway's great
fire of 1894, and I have never found anyone who had met or even
heard of the person described in the ballad, but to call it pure fiction
would be to argue from silence. All we can say is that it does not have
the clear relationship to some historical event that we find in Joe's
other well-known ballads.

That gets us around to the question of just how closely Joe
Scott stuck to the facts of a case when he wrote a ballad. As I have
suggested, he followed the main facts very well, but the details were
apt to take a licking. However, in any discussion of his (or any other
artist's) veracity, we must make the allowance of trying to see the facts
as they would have been known to Joe; it doesn't help our understanding
of the creative process much to know more than he did about what
"really happened." For instance, I have had access to all the available
court records on the Benjamin Deane case and know a good deal more
about what went on than Joe ever did. All he had to go on was what
he read in the newspaper account (and I doubt that he ever saw it),[12]
what he knew about Ben personally (he was very likely acquainted with
him), and what he would have picked up from gossip (which was plentiful
and the usual barroom or "Hell-I-was-right-there" type authorities
(which is where I think he got most of his information). Most of my
official information, however interesting it may be, is irrelevant, but
through interviews with people who were around Berlin at the time
and through careful analysis of the facts reported in the ballad we
can come up with a good picture of what Joe Scott would have known.

Even after we have made such allowances, the fact remains
that Scott distorted and warped reality in his ballads, and these dis-
tortions and warpings are very much in line with the rather simplistic
morality and the plot and character stereotypes of the broadside
ballad world. All the clichés are there: come-all-ye openings, naming
stanzas, the honest parents who reared one tenderly, the idyllic childhood
the mother's good (and not to be followed) advice, the downfall
through greed, whiskey, bad women or all three, pat eulogies, moral

or consolatory closes, they're all in the ballads. In at least three cases we can see Joe taking whole lines and even stanzas from the same ballad he took his tune from, which suggests that he either started with a tune and let the words come to fit it or he chose his tune because something in the words was roughly parallel to the situation he was writing about. It all comes to this: Joe would start with some local event which struck him as the right sort of material for a ballad, then he would fit this event to the exigencies of his models, making what really happened into what should have happened.

"Benjamin Deane" offers a case in point. In this ballad Joe is very careful not to denigrate the character of Lizzie, Ben's wife. Granted that she leaves him and goes off with another man, Joe first shows her pleading with Ben to mend his ways and only leaving him after it was obvious he was not going to change. He always has Deane speak of her as his "fair young wife," whom he dearly loved. That does not seem to be exactly how it was. According to court records there had been trouble between Deane and his wife for at least two years, Deane having had doubts as to her fidelity, and he had ordered her out of the house twice in the days just before the murder. More important for our purposes is what I can reconstruct of the talk that was going around Berlin. It by no means entirely exculpated Mrs. Deane. There was plenty of feeling that it wasn't all Ben's fault, that he had had provocation enough. I am not concerned with trying to establish the "facts" of the case at this point; I only want to make it clear that public opinion showed a rather broad spectrum on just how much justification Deane may or may not have had for shooting his wife. It is all but impossible to imagine that Scott had not heard this uncomplimentary talk about Mrs. Deane; possibly he ignored it because he did not believe it, but I think it is much more likely he did so for artistic reasons. The emphasis he wants is on Deane's downfall, and a loving wife practically driven into the arms of another man by Ben's life of crime suited his purposes. Besides, female murder victims in ballads of this type are notably more sinned against than sinning. If we can't say definitely that Scott *changed* reality here, we can at least say that he was very selective of the material he had available.

Between the limits prescribed by his chosen subject (that is to say, the "facts") and the limits prescribed by the tradition, the folk poet had little room for that "originality," that chance to "offer us something new," which most of us today have come to equate with "creativity." To be sure, he brought to birth something that had not existed before, something that was known to his contemporaries as a "new song," but all that meant was an old tune to new words. Even these "new words" would so closely resemble and were often so clearly modeled on the words to other ballads that it seems monstrously inappropriate to use the word "creation" at all, thereby displaying once again what Eliot described as our modern tendency to "praise a poet upon those aspects of his work in which he least resembles anyone else." Eliot found that orientation limiting, suggesting that "if we approach a poet without this prejudice we shall often find that not only the best, but the most individual parts of his work may be those in which the dead poets, his ancestors, assert their immortality most vigorously."[13] He might lean out from the gold bar of Heaven to sigh a resigned but aristocratic sigh at seeing his words applied to broadside balladry, but certainly we will come closer to understanding such songs if we look for the artistry in the skilful adaptation of traditional elements to new subjects rather than in novelty and experimentation.

But I am defending the obvious, since no one in his proper mind approaches folk art looking for "experiment," "originality," or "contribution." But let's try it. Let's insist on a difference, an individuality. Given a very restrictive tradition in which new effects or wrinkles were not highly valued, can we discover an individual talent at work? Did Joe have a style all his own? Can we hear *his* voice speaking from *his* ballads? Yes, I believe we can, if we are quiet and listen carefully. It speaks from his love of a rather pastoral and conventionalized natural description: bubbling sparkling waters, purling streams, dewdrops bright and fair, roses, moonlight, gentle breezes, "the cuckoo and the swallow, the sunshine and the rain." It speaks also from the frequent contrasts of beauty and violence, such as Benjamin Deane's last look at his wife, "the sun shone through the window on her cold and lifeless face," or, immediately following Guy Reed's horrible death,

"They rolled those logs so carefully
from off his mangled form,

> The birds were singing sweetly and
> the sun shone bright and warm."

It is not a loud voice, and I would not make an attribution on the basis of style alone, but if in listening to a ballad I heard what sounded like Joe Scott's voice, I would certainly look hard for other evidence that the work was indeed his. I should add, by the way, that this is not my judgement only. Several traditional singers have pointed out this special quality. "Joe loved the birds and the flowers," they say to me, or, "He was always putting in something about babbling brooks and purling streams, wasn't he?" Of course, this is often a *post hoc* matter; the speaker knew a ballad was by Joe Scott before he made this pronouncement, but I've heard if often enough to make it worth remarking here.

Up to now I have stressed the role of the poet, but since Joe was obviously one of those poets who wanted his songs to be sung by others, the individual creation was only the beginning of a process. Once created, the song had to be sung and passed on, which is to say it had to be accepted into oral tradition. A quick look at the statistics will show that some of Scott's songs caught on while others did not. Why? To paraphrase Kittredge, there are reasons but there is no reason. Thus "The Grand Trunk Wreck" was probably too abstract and lacked any direct human drama, but "Norman Mitchell" was written long after the years when Joe was an active salesman of his own ballads. On the other hand, once a ballad had been accepted into oral tradition, what is the evidence for what Phillips Barry called communal re-creation, "the summation of an infinite series of re-creative acts?"[14] Plenty, and the changes are of all the expected types, from simple changes on the word and phrase level to stanza inversions, fusions, shifts in tune, all the way up to story changes (albeit nothing very radical). We will have a good deal more to say about this whole matter in the second part of this paper, but one change deserves special mention here. "You know how Joe Scott was always putting in about the bubbling brooks and the flowers and stuff?" remarked Roy Lohnes of Andover to me before going over a ballad he knew. "Well, the whole first of this song was like that, so I just never bothered to learn that part." Considered in the light of what I have already said about Scott's special style, it would seem that the tradition had only limited tolerance for novelty. Nonetheless, nothing that I have found has given much support to the idea that it is this process of oral tradition (with its concomitant of communal re-creation) through which an individual creation becomes remade into a true folk ballad.[15] It would be ridiculous to claim that the individual links in the chain of tradition won't make their influence felt, and it is quite clear that occasionally such a change will be extensive enough to make the line between "creation" and "re-creation" pretty tenuous. But the individual poet, not the process of oral transmission, is the primary alembic. Through him the world and the tradition are transmuted to form the ballad, familiar yet forever new. He himself may be forgotten, almost certainly will be in fact, and his ballad, if it is successful and enters oral tradition, will undergo continual and exciting change. But what it is it is from the beginning, and it is he, the poet, who gives it its identity, its whatness.

What part did Joe Scott's ballad-making play in his life? We will see that more plainly once we have discussed two other aspects of his career closely related to it: his singing and his song-peddling. All his life, Joe was known as a splendid singer.*"I've heard Joe Scott sing, for God's sake!" said Leland Nile of Rangeley with conviction and enthusiasm. "And he could sing too! And he didn't have to--hell, he'd sit right down. He wouldn't bother with anything, you know. Sit right down and sing them right off!" Uncle Joe Patterson of Caledonia, Nova Scotia, told William Doerflinger the following anecdote which, for all its oddness, makes the point well:

> We was in Summit Landing, Maine. The roads was snowed in and the agent at Bemis, three miles down the line, called up for company. He happened to say to the foreman, "I heard some of your boys singin' one day over the phone. Sounded all right."
> "Well," says the foreman, "I'll get ye some singing," and he called Joe and Joe sang

"The Plain Golden Band" over the telephone.
Agent said it sounded just like a talkin' machine.[16]

Before moving on, I wonder if the songmaker isn't always a performer too. Obviously plenty of people could be active tradition bearers yet not creators of new songs, but I suspect that very seldom is the creator not also an active tradition bearer.

Second, Joe made a business of peddling his songs. He was a common sight around the lumbercamps of western Maine. He'd come into a camp with his grip full of printed ballads, spend the evening singing and selling his songs, and then the next day he'd be off for another camp. Many men recall buying songs from him. George Storer of Rumford remembers that Joe had his songs printed on sheets of paper about three feet long, *"...and then if you wanted one or two songs, he'd cut them out for you, see, off'n this long [sheet] .... As I remember it he'd get ten cents apiece for them. . ." Thus we see Joe Scott as a sort of wandering minstrel of the kingdom of spruce, making his headquarters in Rumford Falls and traveling from camp to camp with his little grip full of ballads. He was unique in this respect too. I can find no reports of anyone else in western Maine or anywhere in the northeast who used to do quite what Joe did.

And it is in this uniqueness that we can find one explanation for the popularity of Joe's ballads. To begin with, song always had been an important part of lumbercamp life, there having been specific traditional occasions for, and a healthy interest in, its performance, and this pattern was certainly reinforced in Maine by the influx of P. I.'s and other singing provincemen in the late 19th and early 20th centuries. At just this time, Joe Scott went into these camps and sold his ballads. He sold an honest product, but I think it is even more important that he sold it right where the action was, and he had almost no competition. I don't claim that they explain everything, but these circumstances certainly didn't hurt in getting Joe's ballads as well known as they are.

All the reports I have of Joe's song peddling come from right around the turn of the century, and if we look at the dates we can assign to his ballads an interesting parallel emerges: all of his best-known ballads seem to have been written within about a five year period, three of them ("Howard Carey," "Guy Reed," and "Benjamin Deane") within one year. Of course, I am making an assumption that the ballads appeared soon after the events they chronicle, an assumption which may only be partly correct, but under any circumstances there doesn't seem to be much reason to doubt that almost all of Joe's ballads appeared between 1896 and, say, 1901. It also appears that he began writing rather suddenly. The very fact that there are at least two legends telling how come he took to songmaking in the first place suggests that his contemporaries felt that something was needed to explain why Joe Scott, an otherwise normal woodsman, would start writing and peddling songs.

But if he began suddenly, and once started went at it intensely, he didn't stay with it for very long. Not that he quit entirely; it's just that after 1901 we can see a new emphasis developing. He was still known as a fine singer and as the man who had written "The Plain Golden Band," to be sure, but over the next ten or twelve years we hear less and less about Joe Scott the songmaker and more and more about Joe Scott the magician, the clairvoyant, the worker of wonders. He could do marvelous tricks, find lost or hidden objects, throw his voice, make a table rise into the air, tell fortunes, and toward the last of it he seems to have been studying hypnotism. Some people looked on all this with amusement: it was just fun-loving Joe Scott. Others took a more sombre view. One man, who had heard *"that there were things he could do," noticed Joe was always reading certain books and stole a look at one of them one day and saw *"a lot of black cats...with a lot of reading around them," and he put the book down quickly. Even after sixty years he didn't like to talk about it. *"He had to give himself away, didn't he, for a black art book? Give his soul away?... He just give himself to the Devil, you might say... Oh I don't know for sure you know. But this book, when I see'd that, I knowed it was different from religion, *our* religion, that's all." Even members of the family had heard about Joe's being a "wicked" man who had been involved in "unholy practices." As I have said, he didn't stop making songs entirely. "Norman Mitchell" came as late as 1909, but there is no doubt that the creative energy that churned out the ballads of the late nineties had either largely spent itself or was finding its expression elsewhere–mostly in a sort of sleight-of-hand showmanship, but partly, perhaps, in darker matters.

    Joe Scott was no Larry Gorman. For Gorman, nothing was as important as his songs unless it was being *known* as "the man who makes the songs." In either case, his songs were at the center of his life, and, it turns out, the only thing he did well. Songmaking was just one of the skills Joe Scott was blest with, but at one point in his life there was nothing he was like a Poet. He was "The Celebrated Joe Scott," turning stuff out like billyho and marketing his product with energy and imagination. He probably stayed with it longer than he ever stayed with anything else in his life, but in a life that was sardined with semidesperate unsuccesses that isn't really saying much. He was a dreamer, a maker of great plans, a fast starter, but he had no staying power at all. Even in the lumberwoods, a way of life that seemed made to order for the footloose, even here Joe was known as a wanderer, a woods tramp. When he went back to farming, he cleared a whole lot of new land, and built a big chicken house, then left before he planted a crop or even bought a chicken–left only to become something even more unlikely: a peddler of sewing machines along the upper St. John River. Back around Rangeley he talked about going up to Canada and opening sporting camps. Unable to interest anyone else, he went to northern Quebec, started a homestead, and was back at Rangeley in about two years. That was the last of it, though; the darkness closed in, and whatever it was that drove Joe on went with him wherever he has gone. All his life he kept it hidden beneath the happy-go-lucky redhead, full of fun and jokes, who yet kept his distance, his reserve, so that no-one knew him well. Perhaps old Emma Merrithew, Joe's cousin and just seven years his junior, shows she knew him as well as anyone could:

> *Sometimes when you'd think about him, [*she said*] I think he was planning for something he didn't quite have or didn't, couldn't get. He was planning to do things that maybe he couldn't ever attain to the heights that he wanted to . . . It seemed to be some-

thing he was reaching for. I always thought he was reaching for something he couldn't get. [*You*] wanted to make of him and be so nice with him, you know, and he just had the laugh and smile and the pat on the back and you never could get near him like to sit down and talk to him because he had something else on his mind.

II

The first section of this paper has been largely made up of generalities, not only about folksong and folk poets but also about Joe Scott himself. What I would like to do now is see if we can illustrate some of these generalities by zeroing in on just one of Joe's ballads, "The Plain Golden Band," and discussing it in some detail. I choose this ballad partly because without any question it is the one Scott is best known for, partly because it has the added fascination of being autobiographical. We'll begin with the sad story itself as I have been able to reconstruct it. Next we will see how Joe made his sorrow into a ballad. And finally we will examine what has happened to it as it has passed along from one singer to another. But before we do anything else we should take a look at a good solid traditional version of it, and for that I will turn to my old friend Jim Brown of South Branch, Kent County, New Brunswick.

It was August of 1959, and Jim, who had come up to sing in the Miramichi Folksong Festival, was staying at Tommy Whelan's down in Chatham. We were sitting in Tommy's front parlor, a bottle of rum between us, and Jim was singing some wonderful songs about Waterloo and life in the lumberwoods. Though he was in his seventies, his voice was strong and his style, though thoroughly traditional, was one of the most indidivual I had ever heard, a sort of pulsating staccato that made a line sometimes sound as though there were rests between each syllable. He sat there, thumbs in galluses, rocking back and forth a little, sometimes reaching slowly up to scratch the back of his head. His face was an intense mask, but every so often he'd smile, not at anything in the song but all to himself, as though he were just plain glad to be singing. And he did love to sing. I don't think he was ever happier than when he was singing. That afternoon he sang "The Plain Golden Band" for me. And I was glad to be listening.

THE PLAIN GOLDEN BAND[17]

1.
Oh I been thinking today love on the days past and gone,
As the sun glimmered over the hilltops at morn;
And the dew drop from heaven like diamonds did glow,
They were kissing the roses in the valley below.

2.
Oh the clear purling waters so mild and so blue,
And the green drooping willows where the birds sang so true;
Where the wild roses bloomed on the rocks by the shore,
Where I parted with Lizzie, the girl I adore.

3.
She was lovely and fair as the roses in spring,
She appeared like some goddess or some Grecian queen;
Far fairer than the lilies that had bloomed on the shore,
She's the pride of the valley, the girl I adore.

4.
The day that we parted I ne'er can forget,
For I in fancy I see those sad tears falling yet;
How my poor heart did ache and in sorrow did ring,
When she drew from her finger that plain golden ring.

5.
Saying, "Take back the ring which I fain would retain,
For wearing it only has caused me pain;
I have broken the vows which we have made on the strand,
So take back I pray you that plain golden band."

6.
"Oh renew the engagement, fair darling," I cried,
"Remember you promised you'd be my bride
My love it was true and ne'er can grow cold,
Retain, I beseech thee that plain band of gold."

7.
"Oh dear laddie, I know that your love it was true,
I know that you've loved me and that I have loved you;
And I know you deceived me that night on the strand,
When you placed on my finger that plain golden band.

8.
"On a clear starry evening as the moon it shone bright,
All nature was wrapped in its rich mellow light;
When a gentle cool vapor blew o'er the wild moor,
As I strayed from my cottage to roam on the shore.

9.
"Oh a young man appeared and him I knew well,
He told me false stories, false stories of you;
He vowed that he loved me and offered his hand,
Then I put a stain on your plain golden band."

10.
"Fare you well my fair darling, fare you well and adieu,
Although you've deceived me, it's to you I'll prove true;
Some day think of one while you are roam on the strand,
That has placed on your finger that plain golden band."

11.
Oh she fell in my arrums and cried in despair,
While the gentle breeze ruffled her dark wavy hair;
And the sunlight from heaven shone on her fair hand,
And the same light shone bright on the plain golden band.

12.
"Oh forgive me, forgive me, fair darling," she cried,
"E'er they lay me to rest in some cold silent grave;
And a fond cherished letter penned by your own hand,
Lay 'em on my bosom with the plain golden band."

13.
In some green shady forest [though in] far far away,
Where the deer loves to ramble and the child loves to play;
While all in its nature though it seems wild but grand,
The author you'll find to "The Plain Golden Band."

Kipling's "Conundrum of the Workshops" has special poignance for folklorists, for the Devil always whispers at about this point, "It's pretty, but is it a folksong?" Without getting involved in a full-dress definition of folksong, I can at least point out that authorities have differed. "There are some songs that are so obviously folksongs that a fellow can't very well mistake them for anything else, such as The plain golden band which is of Nova Scotian origin," wrote George Hirdt of Nouvelle, Quebec, to Robert W. Gordon back in 1927 when he sent Gordon a copy of the song along with several others.[18] But Hirdt's instinct was at variance with that of at least one noted collector, Dr. Helen Creighton, who wrote me back in 1957 that she had heard the song but had been "doubtful if it was actually a folk song."[19] In addition, G. Malcom Laws, the ballad scholar and canonist, had misgivings about it, being very skeptical of William Doerflinger's claim that it had been "composed by a New Brunswick logger,"[20] though he later included it as number H-17 in his revised edition of *Native American Balladry* under the rubric "Ballads on Various Topics." At this point in time we can see that Gordon's unlettered correspondent was correct, and we can pick up our lead from Laws and ask just what evidence there is for the claim that Joe Scott did in fact write "The Plain Golden Band."

First of all, we have a printed version of it, a slip, with his name on it. It was given me by Mrs. David Severy of Gray, Maine, who was given it by Joe himself. She knew him well, since she was the younger sister of Lizzie Morse, the heroine of the ballad. The song is neatly printed on a slip of cheap paper 3 3/8 by 11 5/8 inches; at the bottom, in small capitals is "BY JOE SCOTT" and below that, in line with the left-hand margin, "Price 10 cts." It is obviously a sample of the wares Joe sold throughout the woods, and just about as conclusive a bit of evidence as we should need of his authorship. Yet there is more. It is attributed to him more often than any other single song, both by people who knew him well and by people who knew no more about him than that "he was the man who made up 'The Plain Golden Band.'" Many of these attributions are based on reports of Joe Scott's own claim. Peter Jamieson's story is typical, if a bit dramatic. He had left his home in Bathurst, New Brunswick, to work in the woods for Henry and Co. in the Lincoln Valley in New Hampshire, where he met Scott. "After knowing him about a month," he wrote, "one night as him and I were talking one of our crew started to sing The Plain Golden Band. He stopped talking to me, and as I turned to look he was sobbing and tears running down his cheeks. After a while he turned to me and said, 'I am the author of that song and you have found me right where the song said you would. Still true to the vows I made. . ."[21] Finally, as Mr. Jamieson's statement suggests, the song fits perfectly with the facts of Joe's life. Doubts seem to be academic at this point.

Not that I haven't seen counterclaims of sorts. B.H. Rix of Kamloops, B.C., sent in a version of the ballad to *The Family Herald's* "Old Favourites" column. There is no date on the covering letter, but external evidence would place it in the mid forties, and it included this note:

> I was quite surprised and pleased to see in your old favorite page to see Joe Scott's Plain golden band in print again must be getting popular never had any idea it would be when Joe and I composed and wrote it together and sang it many times, out in that logging camp on Beaver Brook in Northern New Hampshire of course Joe was the better half. But there I've gone and done it and told you my secret I've kept locked up for years. . . your correspondent who wrote and sent you Joes song got his wires crossed some not bad I'm sending you Joes song as we wrote it I should know as I had a finger in the pie as some people say.

To be sure, Rix is not saying he wrote the song, merely that he helped Joe and that could mean anything from suggesting a minor change in wording on up. Fred Campbell said that his older brother Alec told him *he'd* helped Joe write "The Plain Golden Band" one winter in the woods up near Bemis. Joe would make up the verses in the woods during the day; then at night Alec would help him write them down, he said. When I asked him what that meant, Campbell wasn't sure but said that was what his brother had told him anyhow. Once again, it is a vague claim of assistance, not of authorship. So far as I know the only out-and-out claim of authorship was made by Jack Scott of Salmon Arm, B.C., in a letter to *The Family Herald* Dated November 18, 1957:

> I am sending in the words of The Plain Golden Band composed by me on a river drive in Maine in 1902 or 3.

> I gave the song to Joe Scott who put the music to it
> and often sang it. I never saw Scott again...It don't
> matter who composed the song at this date.

I don't think there is any need to take this claim seriously, even though the only argument I can use to refute it is the rather flimsy one that several men claim that they learned the song well before 1900. To sum up, although utterly conclusive hard evidence cannot be produced, I am satisfied beyond reasonable doubt that Joe Scott was indeed the author of "The Plain Golden Band."

In order to study the way in which Joe blended tradition and fact, we should have a version of the song that is as close as possible to what he wrote. We have the original printed slip he hawked around the lumber camps; can we assume it represents the ballad as he originally conceived it? Yes, but I say that with certain reservations. It is possible that the printer mistook Joe's intentions and misrepresented them by rearranging some things to suit himself. It is also possible that Joe thought of the ballad entirely in oral terms and therefore couldn't have cared less how the printer set it down so long as he had a copy of "the words" to sell. I don't know any way of settling whatever doubts we may have on these points, but we can at least say that the printed version had Scott's tacit approval in that he sold it. We should also keep in mind the possibility that he had other printings of the song, though I very much doubt if any of them were earlier than the present one. Keeping these reservations in mind, I still think we are quite safe in assuming that the slip represents "The Plain Golden Band" as Joe Scott meant it to be. What follows is the complete text, *literatim et punctatim*. The stanza numbers in brackets are my own addition for convenience of reference; throughout the rest of the paper, all references will be to the stanza numbers as they appear here:

THE PLAIN GOLDEN BAND

> [1.] I am thinking tonight of the days that are gone,
>   When the sun clambered over the mountain at morn,

When the dewdrops of heaven like diamonds did glow,
Were kissing the rose in the valley below;
[2.] Where the clear waters flowing so mild and so blue,
Where the green willows wave and the birds sing so true,
Where the wild roses bloom on the banks by the shore,
There I parted with Lizzie, the girl I adore.

[3.] The day that we parted I ne'er can forget,
Oh I fancy I see those sad tears falling yet;
My poor heart was sad and with sorrow did sting
When she drew from her finger that plain golden ring.
[4.] "Take back the ring that I fain would retain,
For wearing it only causes me pain,
I have broken the vows that we made on the strand,
Then take back I pray you the plain golden band."

[5.] "Retain the engagement ring, darling," I cried,
"Remember you vowed you would soon be my bride,
My love it is true and will never grow cold,
Retain, I beseech you, that plain band of gold.
[6.] Dear lady, I know that your love it is true,
I know that you love me and that I love you."
"And I know I deceived you one day on the strand,
Then take back I pray you the plain golden band."

[7.] "One fine starry night when the moon it shone bright,
All nature was wrapped in her pale mellow light,
And a soft gentle breeze blew o'er the wild moor
As I strayed from my cottage to roam on the shore;
[8.] A young man appeared and him I well knew,
He told me false stories, false stories of you,
He vowed that he loved me and offered his hand,
Then take back I pray you that plain golden band."

[9.] She threw her arms round me and cried in despair,
While a gentle breeze ruffled her dark wavy hair,

> And the moonlight of heaven fell on her fair hand,
> The fair light shone bright on the plain golden band.
>
> [10.] "Forgive, oh forgive me, my darling I crave,
> E'er they lay me to sleep in a cold silent grave,
> With those found cherished letters penned by your own hand
> And on my cold bosom that plain golden band."
>
> [11.] "Farewell, my own love, farewell and adieu,
> Tho' our vows they are broken to you I'll prove true,
> Sometimes think of one when you roam on the strand
> Who placed on your finger that plain golden band;
> [12.] In a cool shady forest so far far away,
> Where the deer loves to roam and the child loves to play,
> Where all nature is gay and the scenes wild but grand,
> There the author you'll find of the plain golden band.
>
> BY JOE SCOTT
>
> Price 10 cts.

Time and time again I have been told by informants of all stripes and sizes, "That's true, you know," or "That really did happen," or "That was about Joe's own life." The story goes that Joe fell in love with a girl named Lizzie Morse. They were going to get married when Joe came down out of the woods in the spring, but while he was gone a fellow by the name of Sam Learned (pronounced Leonard) stepped in and won her away from him. When Joe came out of the woods that spring she gave him back his ring, and the disappointment almost drove him out of his mind. Others say that this is when he began writing songs--that he had never written them before. Not everyone had the whole story, but if we put together many different versions this was the shape of it. Naturally, I was skeptical of anything so neat and fitting, but the Rumford town records bore it all out quietly and all too eloquently.[22] And so did Lizzie's sister, Mrs. David Severy, née Daisy Morse, of Gray, Maine. Let's take time now to re-create the whole affair as best we can.

Old Matthias Morse had been born in Andover Surplus, but

moved to Brunswick (he was related to the shipyard Morses) and
finally to Rumford with his family well before there was any town at
all at the Falls. He was a carpenter, and when that town began to
grow in wildcat fashion as the paper industry built up there in the early
nineties, he helped to put up many of the new buildings there, including
the hotel.[23] To take advantage of the boom, Mrs. Morse set up a small
restaurant and lodging house, and this is evidently where Joe Scott
stayed when he came to Rumford. Mrs. Severy told the story this way:

> *Joe come in on the train, and my brother,--we
> had a beautiful horse--and he used to take the
> people from the station over to the hotel. . .
> [or] wherever they wanted to go, you know, and
> got paid for it. And Joe came in. He couldn't
> get no place to board. And he asked my brother. . .
> if he knew of anyplace, and he says, "Well, if you
> can't get a place I'll take you home with me."
> And so he come in. And he told Mother, he says,
> "Ain't you got a room," he says. "There's a feller
> out there that I want you to give him a room if you
> got one. . . . He can sleep in my bed, and I'll sleep
> on the couch." And so Joe came in. . . .. They
> brought Joe in, trunk and all. Well, of course all
> of us kids took to him right away, and took to his
> singing.

She recalled his arrival at the house:

> *I remember Mother told me to go up and help
> him hang his clothes up in the closet. I was only
> a kid, ten or twelve years old, and I hung his
> clothes. When he took them out of the trunk, you
> know, to hang them in the closet, they was all just
> so. He had a lot of clothes; he had a trunk full of
> of the nicest clothes. He come from awful nice
> people, Joe did.

The whole Morse family thought the world of Joe, but ten-year-old Daisy worshipped him as only a ten-year-old girl could worship a handsome fun-loving man in his mid-twenties. *"I used to like to comb his hair, you know," she told me. "His hair was curly, and Joe'd lay back on the old fashioned lounge we had and I'd comb his hair and he'd always go to sleep. He was just like a brother to us." Old Matthias enjoyed him too. Joe used to kid him a lot, something Matthias did not always take kindly to, but he liked it from Joe. Then Lizzie appeared on the scene.

She was just about twenty years old, and several people have told me what a beauty she was, much prettier than the picture we have of her: petite (size one-and-a-half shoe), lovely complexion, auburn hair, hazel eyes, *"and the fellows was all after her," said Daisy. "She was a great entertainer. She could carry on a conversation, you know, and everybody would pay attention to her and she used to speak a lot of pieces." She'd been away for some little time, Daisy recalls. *"She was away somewhere waiting on tables someplace or somewheres working in a dressmaker's shop, and she come home. And that's how she got acquainted with Joe."

Joe fell hard--no question in anyone's mind about that. How long they went together before they decided to get married we cannot be sure, but Joe did give her an engagement ring. Then on October 19, 1893, they filed their intentions of marriage with the Town Clerk in Rumford, and five days later (the usual time) they were issued a marriage certificate. But the marriage itself never took place.

At about this point I have to surmise a few discreet conjectures, but what seems to have happened is this: Joe was a woodsman and he had to go up into the camps that fall. He probably wanted to marry Lizzie before he went away, but she wanted to wait until spring. He convinced her to take out the license that fall though, just to sort of seal the bargain. And now imagine Joe Scott lying alone nights in the snoring lumbercamp, the wood chunks falling in the stove and the moonlit wind whirring cold in the spruces overhead. Imagine too Lizzie Morse back where the lights were bright (and Rumford Falls *had* electric lights that winter) and men were plenty. Lizzie was not the kind to let herself be lonely, and Sam Learned was in town that winter. Big, rugged, and flambuoyant, he paid court to Lizzie and swept her right off her feet. Joe came back from the woods that spring, she told him how it was, and that was that. Sam and Lizzie were married a year later, and though the *Rumford Falls Times* correspondent wished them "a happy and prosperous married life,"[24] it didn't work out at all. Lizzie divorced Sam for cruel and abusive treatment in 1897, married Ed Martin, and moved to Massachusetts, where she lived until her death in 1948.

How about the ring, the "plain golden band?" I had always wondered about that, since the description fits a wedding ring better than an engagement ring, yet he calls it an engagement ring in the song. I checked that out with Mrs. Severy and she assured me that that's just what it was, a plain band of gold. She further claimed that when Lizzie tried to return the ring, Joe refused to accept it, insisting that she keep it with her. She did keep it too, but ironically enough her second husband Ed Martin took to wearing it. *"He wore in on his little finger," she said, "and they--we was all in swimming to Old Orchard Beach and the plain golden band went into the ocean. He said he lost it off'n his finger."

*"It all but broke our hearts when she broke up with him," Daisy Severy said, and she remembered that Joe was shaken by it. It isn't hard to believe that Joe was deeply hurt by being thrown over in this way. For whatever wild and irrational action a man might take under such circumstances it would be easy to find plenty of precedent. We will never know just what he did, but there are stories that this was the turning point in his life. *"It ruined poor Joe," Angus Enman of Spring Hill, Prince Edward Island, told me, "he just got to be an old bum after that." Dennis Taylor of Coplin Plantation, Me., was of the same opinion. *"It just simply knocked him out, 'twas all. That was the whole of his trouble; that was probably the whole cause of his insanity," he said, referring to Joe's condition in his last years. Many people have said that Joe used to cry every time he sang "The Plain Golden Band," and given the proper conditions--a few drinks perhaps, and the right crowd--it is only too possible that he did, but plenty of men have told me they've heard him sing it and never saw him cry. "Joe'd been a fast one, I guess," Uncle Joe Patterson told William

Doerflinger, "but this time he'd been burned bad. He was crazy over the girl he wrote the song about, so crazy over her he'd sing it over once, and five minutes later, if another man came into the room, he'd sing it over again. But I guess she was a sly one. She let him down all right. He just made up all that stuff about her saying she was sorry."

The general outlines of the story as Joe tells it are correct, then, and those informants who said that "The Plain Golden Band" was about "something that really happened" were right. On this much the record is clear, but what we've been talking about is for the most part background to the song itself. If we are going to study the transmutation of reality into art, what we need to know is exactly what happened that "day" when Joe and Lizzie parted; what we need are the "and-he-said-and-then-she-said" details, and these we do not and cannot hope to have now. But we can be sure that this poem like any other is a distortion, that the poet has reshaped "what happened" for an aesthetic end. For example, even those who have been most insistent that "the song tells all about it" would not, I am sure, carry that insistence to the point of maintaining that Joe and Lizzie spoke to each other in rhyme or even that the speeches in the song represent their actual words at the time. Thus the point for distortion is made by a reduction to absurdity; the actual words and speeches are adjusted to the requirements of the artistic tradition within which Joe was working. We can make some pretty good guesses at the relationship between these two orders, truth and tradition, as we come now to a closer analysis of the song itself. This will allow us to see not only how good a traditional songmaker Joe Scott was but also wherein he was being most original.

The stanza form that Joe chose is a double form of a very common four-line stanza: triple-time, with four beats to the line (or you can call it a predominantly anapestic tetrameter, if you like). A glance through any folksong collection will show parallels aplenty for the four-line version of this stanza,[25] but very few for the double form, although we do find it in "Bendemeer's Stream." Interestingly enough, the tune that we find to this ballad, which is certainly the one Joe had in mind when he wrote the song, is a four-phrase tune, but we'll have more to say about that later on when we come to discuss the tune and the effects of oral tradition on the ballad.[26]

"The Plain Golden Band" begins with a backward look. The reminiscence, the "I'm thinking tonight" opening, is not one of the most common devices of folksong; in fact it is found more in popular music hall songs like "Blue Eyes" and "Slavery Days."[27] Joe uses it in a much more leisurely fashion than his "sources," if sources they were. In fact, he spends his whole first stanza ([1] and [2]) describing a rather literary landscape seemingly for its own sake, not getting around to the real point of it all until the last line--a sixth of his song simply on the backdrop! Another woods poet, W.N. "Billy" Allen, began his "Banks of the Little Eau Pleine" with a similarly leisurely nature scene, but his imagery is much more concrete, much less pastoral, and not a little tongue-in-cheek:

> One evening last June as I rambled
>   The green woods and valleys among,
> The mosquito's notes were melodious,
>   And so was the whip-poor-will's song.
> The frogs in the marshes were croaking,
>   The tree-toads were whistling for rain,
> And partridge's round me were drumming,
>   On the banks of the Little Eau Pleine.
>
> The sun in the west was declining
>   And tinging the tree-tops with red.
> My wandering feet bore me onward,
>   Not caring whither they led.
> I happened to see a young school-ma'am.
>   She mourned in etc. etc.[28]

Joe's imagery here is, as I have said, more literary, more "beautiful." It is certainly not an accurate description of the Androscoggin Valley just above or just below Rumford Falls, although there were the requisite mountains, flowing waters, singing birds, and probably even some roses and willows. The point is it could be *any* valley, idealized by memory and described in largely traditional terms. It is difficult to pinpoint specific phrases, but "The Rose of Tralee" has the correct tone:

> The pale moon was rising above the green mountain,
>   The sun was declining beneath the blue sea,
> When I strayed with my love to the pure chrystal fountain
>   That stands in the beautiful vale of Tralee.
>
> She was lovely and fair as the rose in the summer,
>   Yet 'twas not her beauty alone that won me,
> Oh, no, 'twas the truth in her eye ever dawning,
>   That made me love Mary, the rose of Tralee.
>
> The cool shades of ev'ning their mantle was spreading,
>   And Mary, all smiling, and list'ning to me,
> The moon thro' the valley her pale rays was shedding,
>   When I won the heart of the rose of Tralee.
>   Though lovely and fair, etc.[29]

Joe's second stanza ([3] and [4]) begins the real business of the ballad; the first half [3] is narrative, the second [4] is Lizzie's first speech. His third stanza ([5] and [6]) is mostly devoted to the narrator's imploring her not to break the engagement. However, in the last two lines, Lizzie explains further, going on in the fourth stanza ([7] and [8]) to tell how she has betrayed him. Once again, notice that we have three full lines of traditional nature imagery, the "wild moor" of the third line being a splendid case in point, since there are no moors, wild or otherwise, within a hundred miles of Rumford. Her plea for forgiveness comes in the fifth stanza ([9] and [10]), after a bit of narrative telling how she fell in his arms and wept. Honesty compels me to point out that Joe shifts the scene from daylight to moonlight, though honesty further compels me to mention that I never noticed the fact until this very moment. The last stanza ([11] and [12]) is devoted to the narrator's final speech. He says good-bye, asks her to think of him and says that he will spend the rest of his days in the forest, which he describes once again in general traditional terms.

    There are several noteworthy things about this song as Joe wrote it. The first we have referred to several times already: the high proportion of natural description, all of it rather generalized, pastoral, and "poetic."

In fact, almost a third of the ballad is devoted to such description. Second, two-thirds of the ballad is dialogue between the two principals, and the only direct ascription we get is in the first line of Joe's third stanza ([5]), although a reasonably careful reading, following Joe's punctuation, makes it perfectly clear who is speaking at any time. It is only when the ballad is sung that any problem arises. More about that in due time.

    The most remarkable thing about "The Plain Golden Band" is the sympathetic treatment accorded to Lizzie herself, because here we find Joe moving well beyond anything offered him by folk tradition, and I don't know of anything quite like it in the popular songs of the day. The "hero" is a perfectly stock figure, the jilted lover remembering the sad occasion of his jilting, but the girl in such songs usually does not come off as well as Lizzie Morse does here. Lizzie weeps, begs forgiveness, says she still loves him, even claims she had been told false stories; in fact, the narrator does everything he can to portray her as a lovely young girl unhappily caught in a emotional crossrip. To what extent, does this conscience-stricken girl, so tearful and full of self-reproach, represent the real Lizzie Morse? Is this the way she really did act or is Joe Patterson right that Scott "made up all that stuff?"[30]

    As I have suggested earlier, there is no way of *knowing* for sure now, but my educated guess is that Lizzie *did* act just about the way the ballad says she did. After all, she had been in love with Joe, and she certainly knew that what she was going to do would hurt him terribly. She probably was still very fond of him, but, bedazzled as she was by big blazing Sam Learned, she had to settle the matter. A breaking-off a "Dear John" scene, always tears at the heart-strings, and this one must have been especially difficult. It would be surprising if an emotionally volatile girl like Lizzie did not at least get in some really vintage weeping, and she probably did a good deal more than that-- probably did pretty much what the ballad says she did. She may have been quite dramatic, may even have enjoyed it (back of hand to forehead, "Ah God! The pain of it all!") But however deep and sincere or however shallow and phony her feelings may have been, they must have been obvious, especially to Joe.

The ballad's content, then, is an interesting blend of the traditional, the factual, and the innovative. The setting--the backdrop, the scenery, and the lighting--is purely traditional, and so is the diction (Lizzie never used the word "fain" nor Joe "adieu," I am sure). Yet through the romantic haze these traditional trappings generate, we are seeing something pretty close to what actually happened. The haze is given a richer glow by two further considerations. First, this is a memory poem. We do not know how long after the event Joe wrote this ballad. It was probably not long after, but it could have been up to three or four years later (the external evidence allows this much leeway). However, we can be sure that memory has gotten in its work of heightening drama and softening outlines. Second, the narrator, the *persona*, is portrayed as a man still in love, and such a man will see the past by the light of the torch he carries. It is artistically irrelevant, I suppose, that Joe himself *was* probably still in love with Lizzie when he wrote the song, but we can be sure that Joe *is* the narrator, that *persona* and poet are one. Thus, in a lush arcadian landscape we see through the aureate air two figures moving. Their gestures are stylized and their speeches mannered, but we can still recognize them as Joe Scott and Lizzie Morse.

If we assume that the slip-sheet represents Joe's original (and I have assumed that), we now know where the whole thing started. This is the form in which Joe Scott sold his song from camp to camp in the upper Androscoggin valley in the late nineties and early nineteen hundreds, and the ballad quickly became a part of the standard repertoire for traditional singers in the northeast. We have discussed its birth and parentage; what follows will be its biography. What has happened to "The Plain Golden Band" in the past seventy years?

I will base this life-history on the fifty-four extant versions of the ballad I have brought together. Since a complete descriptive list of every version can be found in the Appendix, I will confine myself here to a couple of generalities on the quality of the texts. To begin with, thirty-seven are complete and seventeen are fragments ranging all the way from one to eight stanzas (I define a fragment as a version recognized by the *singer* as incomplete). Most of my statistics in the following pages will be based on the thirty-seven complete versions, but the fragments will be discussed where they are relevant. Over half of the complete versions were collected in manuscript form, and we can parallel this with the fact that most of the people who sang the song for me were older people who had not sung this or any other song for many years. We are dealing with an item of remembered, not living culture.

As for geographical distribution, this ballad's tradition is, like all the rest of Joe Scott's ballads, almost entirely confined to Maine and the Maritimes. The exceptions, those versions sent in from British Columbia (BC.1 and BC.2) and the one from New Hampshire (NH.1), are not really exceptional at all; Colebrook, New Hampshire, is about twenty miles out of Maine and is part of the same cultural milieu, and both of the British Columbia informants learned the song in this area. Efforts to locate versions of the song elsewhere, in Michigan or Wisconsin for example, have so far been unsuccessful. Further, the tradition is twice as strong in the Maritimes as it is in Maine and New Hampshire, and it is especially strong in New Brunswick; more oral versions come from that province than from all the other areas put together, and the four best renditions I have collected of it are all from New Brunswick. We seem to have here a Maine-to-Maritimes movement, and while we should remember that Scott also sold his songs in New Brunswick along the Saint John Valley, it is likely that most of the Maritimes versions were brought back from Maine by returning woodsmen. We have, in fact, a number of statements that this is exactly what did happen. But it is also clear that the ballad was pretty well established in *local* Maritimes tradition too. That is to say that while the song may have originally come from Maine, the singer learned it in New Brunswick or on Prince Edward Island. For example, Charles Budge wrote me that he had learned the song locally in Victoria County, Nova Scotia, from a man who "in his younger days worked in the lumberwoods in Maine."[31]

Less that half of the people who knew the ballad (that is, contributed versions of it) knew that it was by Joe Scott. One man told me he thought it was by Larry Gorman (everything gets attributed to Gorman, it seems, by someone), but most singers simply had no more idea who wrote this song than they did who wrote any of the other songs they knew. "I have heard all the songs that you had mentioned in your enquiry," wrote William Bergin of Moncton, N.B., "but lumberjacks never seemed to be very concerned as to the author of the songs they knew."[32] True enough, and even among those who *did* know that the ballad was by Joe Scott, only about a third knew or had heard that it was about his own life. However, these figures should be balanced against the fact that a lot of people who did not know the ballad but had heard it or knew something about Joe identified him as "the man who made up 'The Plain Golden Band.'" For instance, one afternoon I was in Meductic, N.B., only a mile or so down the road from the old Scott farm in Lower Woodstock. I stopped at Cummings Brothers Store for a pie and a bottle of pop, and the conversation got around to what I was doing. When I mentioned Joe Scott's name, Cummings said, "Oh yes. that's the fellow who made up 'The Plain Golden Band.' He lived right up here and that was all about his own life, you know." I looked interested, and the next thing I knew another man, a customer, joined the conversation. 'Yeah, that's what I heard too," he said. "Joe Scott made that up and it was true, about himself." Another customer nodded approval, saying that's how it had been told to him too. These were all younger men and none of them knew the song, but they knew the story. The point is that there is the song and there is the story about the song; they were sometimes known to the same people but we cannot say that the story is in any way an integral part of the song's tradition. Given another generation or so and I am sure the story would have disappeared almost entirely. This is not to say that people would have begun to consider the song a fiction. All the evidence shows that traditional singers usually believe that the songs they are singing are true even if they cannot tell where or when the chronicled event took place, and almost all the people who sang "The Plain Golden Band" for me considered it to be a true song. Joseph Pagett of Markhamville, N.B., for example, told me that he had heard that the song was true and that it had originated in Ireland.[33] Thus we can see that within the short span of seventy years not only was the story behind "The Plain Golden Band" being forgotten but the song was well on its way to becoming just another traditional song, anonymous but "about something that really happened."

What part has print played in the life-history of "The Plain

Golden Band?" The most obvious printed tradition has, of course, been the slip itself--the ballad as Joe Scott wrote it and peddled it. Only three versions are directly from this slip, or rather two in addition to the slip itself. Bert Thorne of Jemseg, New Brunswick, sent a manuscript version to *The Family Herald* on December 16,1946, which he had obviously copied from the slip, although there were a couple of changes, the most significant of which are the change in line 6a of "lady" to "laddie," the change of "moonlight" in line 9c to the more consistent "sunlight," and the omission of line 12b entirely (probably an oversight). Mrs. Lucy Morse of Norway, Maine, sent me a copy (Me.13) which is identical in every way with the slip. Others recall buying the song from Scott, and one woman recalls that he wrote it out for her.

We can be sure that numerous copies of this slip did circulate widely in the northeast, but "The Plain Golden Band" reached an even wider audience through *The Family Herald,* a weekly rural newspaper published in Montreal. Back in 1895 this widely read paper began a new department called "Old Favourites," whose announced purpose was "to provide for readers the words of songs which are out of print or difficult to obtain in ordinary song collections." Readers were advised to clip and preserve this column, for "by doing so they will secure, at no cost to themselves, a very complete collection of the best English poetry."[34] Readers did clip this column too, and anyone who has collected songs in the Maritime Provinces (or probably anywhere in Canada) is familiar with the scrapbook or cigarbox bulging with *Family Herald* clippings. It was a very popular department which not only published songs and requests for songs but also would supply printed or typed copies of songs from its files to people who wrote in for them. If the song had only recently been printed they would advise the reader where to find it, but if it had been printed some time before they would usually send a clipping. Since they published "The Plain Golden Band" four different times in the same form, we can also be sure that any versions they mailed out would have been the same too.

The first request for the song appeared on January 5, 1916; "H.B. (N.B.) would like an old favourite called 'The Plain Golden Band,'" and there were further requests, one from New Brunswick and one from Nova Scotia, on February 8, 1922, and on October 14, 1925, followed by a general appeal on December 28, 1927: "Several requests have been made for the 'Plain Golden Band.' Will someone please supply." Finally the song itself appeared as follows on May 2, 1928, "Supplied by W. Sharpe, Dee Side, Quebec, and others":

THE PLAIN GOLDEN BAND

[1]
I am thinking tonight of the days that are gone,
Where the sun slumbers sweetly on the valley at morn;
And the dewdrops from heaven like diamonds did glow
While kissing the rose in the valley below.

[2]
And the clear waters flowing, so mild and so blue.
There came a low whisper to you I'll be true;
The flowers bloomed brightly upon the dark shore.
When I parted from Lizzie, the girl I adore.

[3]
She was lovely and fair as the roses in June,
She appeared like some goddess or some gracious queen,
Fair as the lilies that bloom by the shore,
She's the pride of the valley, the girl I adore.

[4]
The day that we parted I ne'er shall forget,
I fancy I see those sad tears falling yet;
How my poor heart did ache and with sorrow did ring
When she drew from her finger the plain golden ring.

[5]
Saying, "Take back this ring, which I fain would retain,
For wearing it frequently causes me pain;
Our vows are all broken that we made on the strand,
So take back, I beseech you, this plain golden band."

[6]
"Retain our engagement, my darling," I cried,
"You know that you promised you'd soon by my bride;
My love, it is true, it shall never grow cold,
So retain, I beseech you, this plain band of gold."

[7]
"My darling, I know that your love it is true,
I know that you love me and that I love you;
But you know I deceived you that night on the strand,
When you placed on my finger the plain golden band.

[8]
"One bright starry night when the moon it shone bright,
All nature looked gay in its pale yellow light,
It was there a dark stranger crept o'er the moor,
As I strayed from my cottage to roam by the shore.

[9]
"A young man appeared, and him I well knew,
He told me false stories, false stories of you;
He vowed that he loved me and offered his hand
I placed then a stain on the plain golden band."

[10]
"Retain our engagement, my darling I crave,
E'er you lay me to sleep in my cold silent grave;
With those fond cherished letters in my right hand,
And on my cold bosom the plain golden band."

[11]
In some dark shady forest so far, far away,
Where the deer loves to ramble and the child loves to stray;
Where all nature looks gay, the scene wild and grand,
That's the altar you'll find to the plain golden band.

Eight years later, on May 6, 1936, the same version was printed again; then again on October 6, 1943, this time with a note that it was "By Joe Scott of Bangor, Maine." A little over a month later, (November 24), they published an exerpt from a letter by B.H. Rix of Kamloops, B.C., who said that he had been "working with Joe in a logging camp on Beaver Brook, a tributary of the Magallaway River, when he wrote that song." The ballad was printed once more on December 11, 1946, again with a brief biographical note. As I said, each time the paper reprinted the 1928 version, although they had received at least four others in the meantime. I have frequently found these *Family Herald* clippings in people's scrapbooks, though often enough the people who kept the scrapbooks were not themselves singers. If "The Plain Golden Band" ever appeared in newsprint elsewhere I have no record of it, although a couple of people have told me they are sure they saw it in *The Boston Globe.*

For many people, "The Plain Golden Band" was simply another song they had clipped from *The Family Herald;* for them it was a bit of print, not a song they had heard. Most people I have talked to, though, clipped it because it was already familiar. They had heard it sung ("I remember my father used to sing that a lot") or they had once sung it themselves but had forgotten it or no longer sang at all. Still the important question remains, just how much influence can this *Family Herald* version be shown to have had on oral tradition?

I think we can best answer that question by rephrasing it: can we demonstrate that any singer's version was influenced by the *Family Herald* version? Of course, we have to remember that this influence may run an entire gamut, all the way from the printed version's being the direct source of a singer's words (though I have never had a singer admit he learned the song this way) to its being a simple memory-jogger enough to cause a man to recall the song as he had originally known it. I know of no way to determine how effective the *Family Herald* version may have been as a memory-jogger (though it may *help* to explain why this ballad is well known), but it is comparatively easy to see where it has served as a source, partial or complete, immediate or secondary, since it contains a number of unique details, three in particular. First, there is the second line of stanza two: "There came a low whisper to you I'll be true"; second, stanza eight, line three, has a "dark stranger" rather than a "soft gentle breeze" going o'er the wild moor; and in the final line it is not the "author" but the "altar" you will find to "The Plain Golden Band." For the moment I am not considering the third stanza as diagnostic, since it presents a special problem which we will take up in due time. Using these three details as a base, let's see what we can determine about the influence of the *Family Herald* version on individual extant versions of the song.

Sam Jagoe of Newcastle, N.B., sang "The Plain Golden Band" for me on the morning of August 21, 1959 (NB.2). He sang it again that evening at the Second Miramichi Folksong Festival, and both of these singings were all but identical, the changes amounting to such trivia as "this" for "that." In 1963, and again in 1967, Sam told me that he had learned the song while on a Harvest Excursion to Saskatchewan. That was in 1923, and on the train home he heard a man named Piccard from the Gaspé sing it a couple of times, he said. He got the tune and most of the words from him, but later on he got more words from other people he heard sing the song. Sam claimed never to have seen any printed versions of the song, but his second line of stanza two is "There came a low whisper, 'To you I'll be true.'" Then in stanza eight it is a "dark shadow" that creeps o'er the moor, and in the final stanza he had "That's the altar you'll find to this plain golden band," though it is a little difficult to be sure he isn't singing "awter." Sam stays very close to the *Family Herald* version in several other details too, making it abundantly clear that that version has influenced him either directly or indirectly. And I know Sam has learned other songs from printed sources.

William Doerflinger sent me two manuscript versions (NS.2 and NS.3) he had received from Nova Scotia, both of which show clear evidence of *Family Herald* influence if not derivation. Ethel Hamilton of Dalhousie, N.B., submitted a version (NB.8) from her mother's manuscript book of old songs. Since all three details are present, there need be no question of the source. And Kathleen Campbell submitted a version (NB.11) in 1965 which she said she took down from the recitation of her father, Fred A. Campbell of Arthurette, N.B. Campbell had known Scott well, but when I interviewed him in 1963 he claimed he did not know "The Plain Golden Band." One look at the version his daughter claimed her father "remembered quite well" and recited to her makes it clear that he must have read directly from a *Family Herald* clipping.

When John O'Connor of Hope River, P.E.I., sang the song for me on August 31, 1965, he had a clipping of the May 6, 1936, printing in his hand, which he referred to from time to time, and his rendition not surprisingly showed some *Family Herald* influence (Pl.2). I asked him about the clipping, and he said he had only found it the other day; his wife, who had been cleaning out an old trunk, found a copy of *The Family Herald* with the song in it, and he clipped it. It is interesting to compare this clipping-in-hand singing with a manuscript version Mr. O'Connor had sent me six months earlier, well before he had found the newspaper. The manuscript version was incomplete, as he recognized when he sent it, but it still has traits in common with the *Family Herald* version. Yet O'Connor claimed he had learned the song locally from Gabe Warren somewhere around 1925. What probably happened is this: he did learn the song from Warren but sometime after 1936 he found the *Family Herald* version and occasionally used it to refresh his mind. In later years he did not sing much and the paper got put away, only to be rediscovered in the summer of 1965 after he had written me but before he sang the song for me.

At this point we should take up the problem of the "extra" stanza, extra in that it does not appear in Joe's original. It does appear in the *Family Herald* version but is not at all peculiar to it or to versions that can otherwise be shown to derive from it. When present it usually appears as the third stanza, and in four manuscript versions it is clearly labeled as "chorus," in three of them to be sung after a double stanza and in one presumably after every single stanza. Here it is as it was sung for me by Mrs. Lidelle Robins of Hudson, Maine (Me.3):

> She was lovely and fair like the roses in spring;
> She appeared like some goddess or some gracious queen.
> She was pure as the lily that grows by the shore,
> She's the pride of the valley, and the girl I adore.

Possibly this stanza was written by Joe Scott and left out of the original slip by accident; possibly it was added later by someone else; but I think it most likely that Scott added it himself to later versions that he sang or wrote out for people, intending it to be sung as a chorus after every double stanza. Yet where it did catch on it was sung only as a new third stanza, and since the ballad was already in circulation without that stanza, and since that stanza added nothing significant to the story, it was left out about as often as it was included. However it may have gotten into the ballad, there is no question but that it has become part of the tradition though, as I have already suggested, it is the least stable stanza in that tradition. Of the fifty-four versions of the song I have been working with (a figure that includes all versions, complete and fragmentary), it occurs in only twenty-one and by far the largest number of these are manuscript versions of one sort or another. It occurs in all of those versions influenced by the *Family Herald,* and its occurrence in print certainly helped to spread it around.

One final point should help to make it clear that "The Plain Golden Band" was passed on by a predominantly oral tradition. Had any singer learned this ballad from print without ever having heard it sung, he would have had to supply his own tune, and by all odds that means we would find "The Plain Golden Band" sung to different tunes. We don't. The tune tradition is very stable. And that sums up all we can discover about the influence of print on this ballad's life history. It is a clear but minor influence that has created some interesting eddies in the main stream of oral tradition without changing its course significantly. It remains for us to see now what changes that oral tradition has worked on Joe's original production.

Before continuing, I would like once again to emphasize my assumption that the original printed slip represents "The Plain Golden Band" as Joe Scott meant it to be. One implication of this assumption is that Joe's punctuation and arrangement of lines can give us clues to his intentions, especially since this slip shows every evidence of being carefully printed and punctuated--and so do the slips of three of his other ballads that I have seen. I depend rather heavily on the evidence presented by such details, and quite obviously I believe I am correct in doing so, but it won't hurt to be disarmingly honest about the possibility for error at this point.

To simplify matters, I will refer to the stanzas by the numbers I have given them in Joe's original version on pages 92-94 above. The ballad can be thought of as consisting of four main "movements" or "sections": the introduction (stanzas 1 and 2 plus the "chorus"); the first exchange of speeches (stanzas 3, 4, 5, and 6); Lizzie's explanation (stanzas 7 and 8); and the final exchange of speeches (stanzas 9, 10, 11, and 12).

The first section, the introduction, is found in every version that makes any pretence at even halfway completeness, and only Bill Cramp of Oakland, Maine, got all the essentials into one stanza (Me. 1):

I'm thinking today of the days that are gone
When the sun clambered over the mountains at morn;
Where the bright golden lilies they bloom by the shore,
There I parted with Lizzie, the girl I adore.

However much we may feel such economy to be a virtue, it is obvious that traditional singers of this song enjoyed the lush full treatment. Thirty-one of the thirty-seven complete versions give us both stanzas 1 and 2, and of these eighteen add the chorus as an additional stanza. Only four versions have less than two stanzas, and of these, only Bill Cramp's is very satisfactory. Even when we turn our attention to the fragments, we find that this section has been exceptionally memorable, but we should expect that the first stanza or two of any ballad would be the ones most often remembered (what traditional singer does not have a score of such opening stanzas cluttering around in the back of his mind?). Even when we get down to the details, these two stanzas are amazingly stable. The variations are limited to such small matters as the sun "clambering," "clouring," "climbing," "rising," or "slumbering" over the mountain; and the versions are about equally divided on whether it is a "gracious" or a "grecian" queen (with one vote each for "greater" and "generous") in the second line of the chorus. The only really significant variation in these stanzas is one I have already discussed: the tell-tale "to you I'll prove true" found in line 2b of *Family-Herald*-influenced versions.

The second section, made up of stanzas 3, 4, 5, and 6, comprises what I have called the first exchange: a narrative stanza setting the scene

(3), Lizzie's offer to return the ring (4), his plea that she keep it because he still loves her (5 and 6ab), and her statement that she has deceived him (6cd). No complete version omits this section; at the very least they all get across the idea of the broken vows and the ring being returned. In fact, most of the versions have everything just about as Joe meant it to be, until we come to stanza 6. Here Joe's original intent, as I understand it, has been altered.

The way Joe Scott had stanza 6 printed, the first two lines are a continuation of the narrator's plea in stanza 5 to Lizzie to keep the ring, while the last two are the beginning of Lizzie's explanation of how she betrayed him:

> "Dear lady, I know that your love it is true,
> I know that you love me and that I love you."
> "And I know I deceived you one day on the strand,
> Then take back I pray you the plain golden band."

Now there is nothing unusual about either unintroduced dialogue or about a stanza in which the first two lines are spoken by one party, the last two by another. If fact, such stanzas are quite common in the so-called Child ballads. But it is impossible to sing the present stanza and have it make sense the way Joe Scott intended it to make sense. Try it how you will, it still comes out feeling as though the whole stanza is a single speech, and that is exactly what singers have made of it. All but three of the twenty-seven versions in which this stanza is present have the whole stanza as *her* speech, and of the three that don't one is a direct typed copy of Scott's original slip (Me.13). Most manage this change of sex the way Jim Brown did,[35] by simply substituting the word "laddie" for lady" in line 6a:

> "Dear laddie, I know that your love it is true,
> I know that you love me and that I love you.
> But I know I deceived you one night on the strand
> So take back, I pray you the plain golden band."
>
> (Me.7)

Others have it as "my darling," probably following *The Family Herald's* lead, since almost every one of them shows the influence of that version in other details as well. The important thing is that the process of "communal re-creation" can certainly be said to have improved on the original, at least insofar as it has made something unsingable into something singable. And we don't have to get mystical or theoretical about it all either; from the nature of the stanza it had to happen this way!

The next section, stanzas 7 and 8, consists of Lizzie's explanation of what happened. Only one version omits this section entirely,[36] and of the rest all but three have both stanzas in full. It is amazingly stable in its details, but there are two changes that are worth mentioning. The first is the substitution of the "dark stranger" for the "breeze" or "zephyr" that crosses the moor, and this is one of those changes we find in the *Family Herald* version we have already discussed. The other involves a change in line 8d. Taking it in conjunction with the preceding line, we find that Joe Scott wrote,

> He vowed that he loved me and offered his hand,
> Then take back I pray you that plain golden band.

There is no suggestion that Lizzie did anything but change her mind, but tradition has been harsher on her than Joe would have liked, changing that line to "Then I put a stain on your plain golden band." With the exception of those two versions that derive directly from the original slip, almost every other version has this more suggestive line. Whether it is an "improvement" or not is a matter of opinion, but there is no doubt that this line has replaced Joe Scott's original and the folk have once again had their way. Its occurrence in the *Family Herald* version certainly helped to establish it but it is too widely known to be explained simply as an incursion from print.

At this point I should mention one of the more unusual versions, that sent in to *The Family Herald* by Jack A. Scott of Salmon Arm, B.C., who claimed to be the author of the song. We should remember, however, what Fannie Hardy Eckstorm said: "a woodsman would claim 'Hamlet' if he had added four doggerel lines to the Soliloquy."[37] Here is the way Jack Scott worked out the central sections of the song:

> A young man he came to me one I knew well
> He told me false stories false stories of you
> He vowed that he loved me and offered his hand
> There I put a stain on that plain golden band.
>
> He who made the bold eagle made also the dove
> All the beauty in nature tell of his love
> His kindness and mercy should teach us to live
> To be kind to each other and freely forgive
>
> I know my dear laddie but my vows were untrue
> I knew that you loved me and that I loved you
> I know I deceived you that night on the strand
> So take back I pray you that plain golden band.
>   (BC.2)

Evidently Lizzie speaks the first and third of these stanzas and the narrator speaks the second. It is not an entirely bad touch, but it never caught on at all.

That brings us to the final section, stanzas 9, 10, 11, and 12. It includes a descriptive narrative stanza (9) telling how Lizzie threw herself into his arms and wept; her final speech, a plea for forgiveness (10); the narrator's farewell (11); and his final statement of where he may be found. This is a diffuse section in a pretty diffuse ballad. If there is a trend toward economy in oral tradition, a trend that causes stanzas unnecessary to the story line to be forgotten more easily than others, we should be able to see it operating here if anywhere. Unfortunately, the evidence is equivocal. Take stanza 9, for example:

> She threw her arms 'round me and cried in despair
> While the gentle breeze ruffled her dark wavy hair,
> And the moonlight from heaven shone on her small hand,
> It glittered and gleamed on the plain golden band.
>   (Me.3)

It adds little if anything to the story, being almost entirely lyrical and descriptive, and while it occurs in seventy-five percent of the complete versions it is still one of the stanzas most frequently omitted. But that hardly establishes a trend. On the other hand, stanza 11 is more cooperative, turning up as it does in less than sixty percent of the complete versions:

> Fare you well my own darling, farewell and adieu,
> Though the vows you have broken, I'll always be true;
> Sometimes think of me when you roam on the strand,
> Where I placed on your finger the plain golden band.
> (Me.1)

In my opinion, something is gained by the rather dramatic shift that occurs when it is omitted:

> "Forgive, oh forgive me, my darling I crave
> E'er they lay me to rest in that cold silent grave;
> With those fond cherished letters penned by your own hand
> And on my cold bosom the plain golden band."
>
> Now in the cold shady forest so far far away,
> Where the deer love to ramble and the child loves to play;
> All nature is glad and the scenes wild but grand,
> There you'll find the author of the plain golden band.
> (Me.4)

Traditional singers seem to have shared my opinion, because of the thirty-seven complete versions (not counting Joe's original), twenty end in this way even though in three of them stanza 11 is present earlier in the ballad.[38] That stanza 11 is easily forgotten is further borne out by the fact that it occurs in only one fragmentary version--and that a long one (NB.15). On the matter of a trend toward economy, then, the best we can say is that this section offers some support for it, but it is a very qualified support.

    The final stanza, as we might expect, occurs in every complete version and in over half the fragments. It is always the final stanza too, never occurring elsewhere in the ballad. The only significant variation is the change in line 12d of "author" to "altar," which we find in those versions influenced by *The Family Herald*. But once again we have the question of what Joe Scott seems to have intended as compared with what singers have made of it. If we look at Joe's original version, we find that line 11d has no close-quote and is not end-stopped. Since he seems to have been careful with his punctuation elsewhere, the semicolon here would indicate that he wished us to see the last four lines (that is, stanza 12) as part of the narrator's final speech to Lizzie. In such a circumstance, it is a little difficult to know just how he meant us to construe the final line, but if this *was* his intention then he was once again making a distinction in print that it would be impossible to convey in singing. The whole stanza makes much better sense as an epilogue, a return to the time level of the introduction; then it is not the narrator speaking in time past to Lizzie about where she *will* find him, it is rather the narrator speaking in time present directly to the listener about where the narrator now *is*. In this way the final line makes perfectly good sense too, and I know that this is how most singers I have talked to about it interpret the stanza. When stanza 11 is omitted, and we have just seen it often is, that is the *only* way the final stanza makes any sense. The point I would like to make here is that while Joe Scott's handling of the final stanza as it is represented by the printed slip leaves some doubt about his intentions, there is no question at all about its meaning in subsequent versions. It is an epilogue and that is that.

    Having now completed what amounts to a rough statistical survey, I would say that for a ballad as diffuse and lyrical as "The Plain Golden Band," it is remarkable that so many versions have retained the original structure pretty much intact. Yet I do not want to overemphasize the narrative element in this ballad, because while it is undeniably there the important thing is the overall tone, the general feeling of sadness over the parting of lovers, remembered sorrow in a lovely landscape. Even when all the stanzas are in "correct" order, the singers I have talked to are not always certain how to assign a speech, nor, I must confess, was I until I sat down one day and figured it all out. With a couple of dubious exceptions,[39] I know of no versions that have gone the whole way to becoming lyrics; the story line is present in every version I have that is given as complete, but were I arranging folksongs along a narrative-lyric spectrum, I would place "The Plain Golden Band" toward the center but somewhat on the narrative side.

As I have said, most of the versions follow the original order of stanzas, but there are alternative ways that turn up and still make sense. Stanzas six and nine for example, have a certain free-floating quality about them and may appear at different points in the song. F. L. Tracy of Brewer, Maine, contributed a version (Me.11) in which Lizzie's plea for forgiveness (stanzas 9 and 10) occurs before she tells her story (stanzas 7 and 8), which makes perfectly good sense. And so does the manuscript version contributed by Lloyd Belyea of Brown's Flat, N.B., in which Lizzie asks the narrator to take back the ring (3-4) and tells her story (7-8), whereupon he pleads with her to retain the ring, (5) she says she knows his love is true but she has deceived him (6) and she begs his forgiveness (9-10). But one of my favorite renditions, that of Joseph Pagett of Markhamville, N.B. (NB.16), simplifies the whole thing by being the only version to omit Lizzie's confession. It works out very nicely:

THE PLAIN GOLDEN BAND[40]

A MAN AND HIS SONG

[1]
I'm thinking tonight of the days that are gone,
As the sun clambered over the mountains at morn;
And the dewdrops from heaven like diamonds glow,
While kissing the roses in the valley below.

[2]
'Neath the clear flowing waters so mild and so blue,
Where the wild willows waves and the birds sing so true;
Where the wild flowers bloom by the banks of the shore,
There I parted with Lizzie the girl I adore.

[3]
The night that we parted I ne'er shall forget,
I fancy I see those sad tears falling yet;
My blue eyes were dim and with sorrow did sting,
As she drew from her finger that plain golden ring.

[4]
Saying, "Take back the ring that I vain would retain,
For wearing it causes me sorrow and pain;
The vows they're all broken we made on the strand,
So take back I pray thee that plain golden band."

[5]
She threw her arms around me and cried in despair,
As the gentle winds ruffled her dark wavy hair
And the bright stars from heaven shone on her small hand
And the moon it shone bright on the plain golden band.

[6]
"Farewell, my old sweetheart, farewell and adieu,
The vows they're all broken, to you I'll prove true;
Sometimes think of me when you roam on the strand,
Who placed on your finger that plain golden band."

[7]
In the green shady forest so far far away,
Where the deer loves to roam and the child to play;
All natures seem gay and the scene wild but grand
There the author you'll find of the plain golden band.

Joe Pagett's version does change the story, but since, as I have said, the narrative element is quite subdued in "The Plain Golden Band" to begin with, we can hardly say that any of these changes through omission or changing the order of stanzas makes much difference. Nor can we show that any clear local versions or oicotypes have developed for this ballad, but it is through such changes as we have been describing that oicotypes would presumably develop in time.

Not only is the basic structure of "The Plain Golden Band" surprisingly stable for a ballad so lyrical, but the structure of the individual stanzas is too--so stable that we can speak of the stanza as the basic unit. Of all the stanzas in all the versions, only about six percent are composites like Bill Cramp's opening stanza,[41] and that figure is even lower (only four percent) if we consider only complete versions. Quite predictably, almost all the composite stanzas break at the midpoint: one couplet coming from one stanza, the other from another. But in every case, the first couplet is always from the first part of the stanza, the second from a second part. Probably this has been aided by the fairly consistent rhymes with "band" in the second half of the stanzas. To sum up for now, then, even though we must keep in mind that seventy years is a relatively limited time (we are often dealing with only one link in the chain of oral transmission, and probably never with more than three or four), I would still say that the words to "The Plain Golden Band" have shown an amazing resistance to change.

If the words have shown an "amazing resistance to change," it is hard to know just how to characterize what has happened to the tune. With one exception (Me.15), "The Plain Golden Band" is always sung to the same tune, and it is the only song I have ever found that *is* sung to that tune. It is straight major with a range of a ninth from the second above to the octave below the final (two stretch that to a minor tenth, one of them Joe Pagett's version). The meter is usually 3/4 or 6/8 with an occasional 2/4 or 4/4 infix. Even in those versions sung *parlando rubato* it is still possible to see this basic meter throughout. The phrase pattern is progressive (**ABCD**) and the tune is an undulating one that stays consistently below the final except for those stressed high notes in the second and fourth phrases. All in all, there is nothing in this description that gainsays the tune's traditional quality. As a matter of fact, James Wilson considers it a set of the standard "Villikins and his Dinah" tune, and in conversation Norman Cazden recently suggested to me the same similarity.[42] I can hardly deny that there is a resemblance, but if it is truly in this family it seems to be a sub-family all to itself. The stressed high seconds and the fact that it rises rather than descends to its final particularly seem to set it apart from other versions of this tune. It may well be, then a traditional tune, but I still have suspicions (and that is about as specific as I can be) that it is a late nineteenth century popular tune that Joe heard somewhere.

If my sixth sense if right and this *is* a popular tune, or even if it is the tune to some other traditional song, it is rather remarkable that I have not found the original. I have whistled my way through scores of song collections with no success; I have all but gone hoarse singing it for people who should have recognized anything there was to recognize, only to be rewarded with a puzzled smile, perhaps a statement that it sounds "familiar," and some measure of support for my suspicion that it is a popular tune. I have never collected another ballad sung to this same tune, nor has any traditional singer ever described it as "the tune to such-and-such." Wherever I have found it, it has been the tune to "The Plain Golden Band."

Is it possible that Joe Scott *wrote* this tune? Several people have told me that he did, and we might recall that Jack Scott of Salmon Arm, B.C., who claimed that he himself wrote the words, claimed also that he "gave the song to Joe Scott who put the music to it and often sang it." Since I do not credit Jack Scott's claim to have authored the words, I have no reason to credit his claim that Joe wrote the tune. None of the other attributions are especially authoritative either. But suppose Joe Scott did in fact "write" this tune. What would that mean he had done? Just as with the words, he would have used the patterns and formulae that his tradition offered him and would probably have come up with a tune that sounded very much like many others while yet being distinct from them. He may have deliberately made up a new tune without being in any way aware that all he was really doing was making a variation on a tune he already knew, the well-known "Villikins and His Dinah." But I don't think this is what happened. As a rule, songmakers took an old tune and created new words to it, and I see no reason to believe that Joe Scott was any exception. It would certainly be ridiculous to assume that he wrote this tune merely because I have not been able to find his source, be it folk or popular. We cannot prove that he wrote it and I doubt that he did. But it is just possible. We'll have to leave it at that.

There is still one more matter to be dealt with in our consideration of the tune. I pointed out earlier that Joe's original version of the words is printed in an eight-line stanza form while the tune has only four phrases.[43] Could Joe have had a different tune in mind, one with eight phrases, when he wrote the song? The Irish tune for "Bendemeer's Stream" or "The Mountains of Mourne" would fit perfectly, for example, and there is that intriguing coincidence (unless it *is* echo, which I doubt) of the latter title in the second line, where it speaks of the sun coming over "the mountains at morn." "The Rose of Tralee" would (with a little shoving) fit too. Eight-phrase tunes frequently break down in oral tradition into two four-phrase tunes, and often only one of the two will be used in some versions of the song. It is possible that something like this could have happened to "The Plain Golden Band," but I think it is highly unlikely. For one thing, whenever we find an eight-phrase tune that has become a four-phrase tune, we usually find versions of the song that use the eight-phrase tune too.[44] This we never find with "The Plain Golden Band." It is always sung to the same four-phrase tune. Then too, I have talked with a number of people who have heard Joe Scott himself sing the song, and none of them have ever made the point (even when I asked about it) that he sang it to a different tune than the one we hear today. I am positive that the tune we have to this ballad is the one Joe Scott meant to be there. Whatever his reasons may have been for having the song printed in six eight-line stanzas rather than twelve four-line stanzas, he was once again making a distinction in print that it would be impossible to convey in singing, and while some of the manuscript versions have kept the eight-line stanzas none of the oral versions do. Those who sang the ballad can be said, then, to have worked a change, though it is again more a change in how the singer sees or hears the song in his head than it is a change through omission, addition, or alteration of material.

It is time for a summing up of this study of "The Plain Golden Band." Joe Scott is plainly the author, and he made the song up somewhere between 1894 and 1898 in the upper Androscoggin valley. He had the song printed and sold copies of it around the lumbercamps of the region; then at a later date, probably not much later though, he added a chorus. While the imagery, speeches, and general tone are highly conventional and romantic, nevertheless the ballad stays very close to what actually happened. "The Plain Golden Band" has become part of standard traditional repertoire all through Maine and the Maritime Provinces, where often as not it has become just another anonymous but "true" ballad. Joe's printed slip and four printings of the version in *The Family Herald* have left a clearly identifiable mark on it. While the structure of both the overall story and the individual stanzas has remained remarkably stable for a ballad so lyrical, nevertheless there is clear evidence that the folk have re-worked it in several ways, especially in those places where Scott's printed distinctions could not be maintained in singing. The tune we always find is almost certainly the one Scott put to it, and while he may have written it himself it is more likely derived from a popular song of the time.

*   *   *   *   *   *   *   *

A man and a song. Joe Scott moved through the world for a little while, and now both he and the world he knew are gone. But the song goes on. Life is brief and even art is not long but sometimes it is longer than a man. It is in the nature of things that a folk poet will be forgotten, but we are lucky enough to have a few names: Billy Allen, Orville Jenks, John Calhoun, Jack Thorp, and the Reverend Andrew Jenkins, for example.[45] Like Joe, all of them put ballads into oral tradition; we can grant them that common clay. But they are not like Joe, and they are not like each other. Before we emphasize their similarity, let us try to see each one in all his individuality--counter, original, spare, strange. Let us watch each one working with a unique endowment under unique circumstances within a common tradition. Then let us follow each song as, entering life after life, it grows and changes yet remains the same--continually becomes yet always is what it is. And from the study of all this diversity may we come in time to a better understanding of creativity, and of what a tradition really is.

LIST OF VERSIONS USED IN THIS STUDY

Note: Items marked ATL are in the Archives Tape Library of the Archives of Traditional Music, Maxwell Hall, Indiana University, Bloomington, Indiana, with copies in the Northeast Folklore Archives. Items marked NFA are on file in the Northeast Folklore Archives, South Stevens Hall, University of Maine, Orono, Maine.

FH   First published in *The Family Herald,* May 2, 1928, "Supplied by W. Sharpe, Dee Side, Quebec, and others." Reprinted May 6, 1936; October 6, 1943; and December 11, 1946. 11 sts. w/o tune.

JS   Original printed slip, collected from Mrs. David Severy, 83, Gray, Me. July 21, 1966. 12 sts. (or 6 d.sts.) w/o tune.

Me.1   Bill Cramp, 83, Oakland, Me., Oct. 1964, collected by George Keller; NFA Tape 225.1, Ms.225.21. Sung and recited; 10 sts. w/tune. Knew it was by Joe Scott and about his own life. Sang all but the last two stanzas, which he recited. But then said that these two stanzas were so good that he wanted to sing them, and he did.

Me.2   Omer McKenna, Rumford, Me., c.80, September 28, 1965; collected by E.D.I., NFA Ives tape 65.19; fragment, 2 sts. w/tune. Knew it was by and about Joe Scott.

Me.3 Mrs. Lidelle Willey Robbins, c.70, Hudson, Me., assisted by Vera Robbins (her daughter-in-law), February 8, 1957; collected by E.D.I., ATL 2138.11, 11sts. w/tune. Learned from her brothers who used to work in the woods. Knew it was by Joe Scott. Mrs. Robbins had dictated the words some weeks before to her granddaughter, who typed them out. Mrs. Robbins was too nervous to sing alone, so her daughter-in-law sang along with her. Only stanzas 1-3 sung; rest in manuscript.

Me.4 Ray Lohnes, c.70, Andover, Me., July 1958; taken down from recitation by Miss Anna Thurston; 10 sts. w/o tune. Lohnes knew the song was both by and about Joe Scott.

Me.5 Gordon Frazer, c.72, Caribou, Me., September 19, 1962; collected by Lorina Wakem, NFA Ms.412.49; fragment, recited 1 1/2 sts. w/o tune. Learned about 1914 up on Chase Brook from Christopher Columbus Davenport. Same item collected from same man by Marion Porter, NFA Ms. 320.61.

Me.6 Mrs. Gertrude Bradbury, Mexico, Maine, written down from recitation by her daughter, Mrs. Pearl Longley, in a notebook loaned to me September 29, 1965; 9 1/2 sts. w/o tune. Knew it was by Joe Scott. Mrs. Longley had begun writing her mother's songs down shortly before her death some years before I met her. Mrs. Bradbury had lived most of her life around Monticello and her husband had worked with Joe Scott on the Bank Farm near there.

Me.7 Evelyn Smith, Rangeley, Me., a manuscript version taken from the singing of Bob McKinnon, about 1925. Collected by Lillian Williams, Rangeley, Me., April 1960, NFA Ms.414.46-50. 12sts. w/o tune. Both McKinnon and Smith knew it was by and about Joe Scott.

Me.8 Bessie Lary, Dover-Foxcroft, Me., manuscript sent me June 13, 1964; 11 sts. w/o tune. Miss Lary's note: "This is a copy by

Fred L. Barrows, Oakfield, Maine, (deceased)." Did not know it was by or about Joe Scott.

Me.9   Mrs. Jerry Desmond, Island Falls, Me., and sent by mail to Helen Hartness Flanders, July 19, 1940. Her husband, Jerry Desmond, sang it for Flanders Collection, cylinder C-211.

Me.10 Dennis Taylor, 85, Green Farm (Coplin Plantation), Me., March 30, 1959. Collected by E.D.I., NFA Ives tape 59.1. Taylor had known Scott and knew this song was by and about him. He recited it as a kind of rhythmic prose. Fragment.

Me.11 F.L. Tracy, Brewer, Me., manuscript sent in to Fannie Hardy Eckstorm, February 19, 1934. Eckstorm Papers, 12 sts. w/o tune. Written on the sheet in F.H.E.'s hand "probably composed by Joseph Scott, of Androscoggin region, who sold printed songs to woodsmen about 1900."

Me.12 Elwell Field, Westfield, Me., November 19, 1962. In manuscript. Collected by Beatrice Field, NFA Ms.128.39-41, 13 sts. w/o tune. "Bill Hallett sang it on Burntland Stream in 1911." Did not know it was by or about Scott.

Me.13 Mrs. Lucy Morse, c.80, Norway, Me. Typescript sent to me, Sept. 23, 1966. 12 sts. (6 d.sts.) w/o tune. Knew it was by and about Scott. This version is identical in every way with Scott's original slip.

Me.14 Edward Gavel, c.70, Sanford, Me., August 25, 1965, collected by E.D.I., NFA Ives tape 66.11; 1 st, w/tune. On Oct. 3, 1966, he sent me a manuscript copy of all the words he could recall; 9 sts. w/o tune. Fragment.

Me.15 Wilbert Morrison, 77, Orland, Me. Fragment collected by Mrs. Bonita Ede, January 9, 1969, her tape number 69.1. 3 sts. w/tune. Says he learned it locally. Mrs. Ede asked him in November if he knew this song, and he said he'd have to put it together. The tune he sings begins like "When You and I Were Young, Maggie," but never really settles down into being anything. My impression (and Mrs. Ede's) is that he did not really remember the tune at all, but put this together to oblige her.

NH.1   Mrs. Belle Richards, Colebrook, N.H., November 21,1941; collected by Marguerite Olney for Flanders Collection, D-316; 11 sts. w/tune. Someone prompting her at the beginning, but no indication who or from what.

NH.2   C.S. Locke, 90, Berlin, N.H., September 9,1965; collected by E.D.I. NFA Ives tape 65.14. Fragment, 1 st. w/tune. Locke had known Scott, and knew this song was by and about him.

NB.1   James Brown, 76, Chatham, N.B., August 20,1059. Collected by E.D.I. ATL 2183.3; 13 sts. w/tune. Believes he got this written down from someone and learned it from the written copy. Originally thought it was by Larry Gorman. Mr. Brown is from South Branch, Kent Co., N.B., but was staying with Tommy Whelan in Chatham while he attended the Miramichi Folksong Festival. This version given above, pages 87-89.

NB.2   Sam Jagoe, 62, Newcastle, N.B., August 21, 1959; collected by E.D.I., ATL 2185.2; 11 sts. w/tune. See p. 109 above for more complete data. For Jagoe's second singing of it, see ATL 2201.6 (see Manny and Wilson, p.164-65). For the tune to an earlier singing, see Doerflinger, p. 247.

NB.3   George Duplessis, c.60, Newcastle, N.B., September 15,1958, at First Miramichi Folksong Festival; collected by E.D.I., ATL 2176.6; 12 sts. w/tune. Duplessis comes from Eel River Bridge, N.B.

NB.:4   William J. Bergin, Moncton, N.B., manuscript sent in a letter to me of June 21, 1964, as recited by a young man named

Vincent Cashen, Blissfield, N.B., and taken down by Bergin's sister at least forty years before; 12 sts. w/o tune. Did not know it was by Joe Scott. Written down without any breaks between stanzas.

NB.5 Gordon Mountain, Blackville, N.B., as written down by Hugh U. Crawford and given to me June 9,1957; 11 sts. w/o tune.

NB.6 John A. Jamieson, 85, East Bathurst, N.B. Words as sent in to *Family Herald,* no date given but probably early 50's. Tune collected by E.D.I. in East Bathurst, June 12, 1957, ATL 2153.7; 12 sts w/tune. "I learned this song over 50 years ago in Lincoln, N.H., by a man who knew Joe Scott, the author," (J.A.J. in note to *Family Herald.*)

NB.7 Peter Jamieson, 75, East Bathurst, N.B. in a letter to me of March 4, 1957, 11 sts. w/o tune. Had met Joe Scott and knew it was by him. Source of manuscript version not clear.

NB.8 Mrs. Margaret Hamilton, River Charlo N.B.; copied out from her notebook and given to me, July 24, 1965 by her daughter, Ethel Hamilton, NFA Ms. 194.26-27; 11 sts. w/o tune. "Another of the songs my mother had written out years ago." See above p. 109.

NB.9 Thomas Cleghorn, 86, Harvey Station, N.B. Words from a typed copy given me by his daughter, Mrs. Karl Byers, Harvey Station, August 22, 1964; 13 sts. (6 d.sts. w/chorus) w/o tune. That same evening Mr. Cleghorn sang 6 sts. from the typescript; NFA Ives tape 64.6. Had known Joe Scott and knew this song was by and about him.

NB.10 Ansel Libby, c.65, Lower Woodstock, N.B., August 22,1964; collected by E.D.I., Ives tape 64.4; fragment of 6 sts. w/tune. Learned in northern Maine from the singing of a man named Norman McDold, a sailor who was putting in that winter in the woods. Knew the song was both by and about Joe Scott. Says he has seen this song printed in the *Boston Globe* with Scott's name to it. Mr. Libby was simply singing what he remembered of it at my request. He is married to Scott's niece, and we were sitting in the parlor of the old Scott homestead.

NB.11 Fred A. Campbell, 82, Arthurette, N.B., June 17,1965; collected by his daughter, Kathleen Campbell, NFA Ms.80.49-51; 11 sts. w/o tune. See above p. 109 for a discussion of this version.

NB.12 Fred Anderson, c.55, Juniper, N.B., October 9,1965; collected by E.D.I., Ives tape 65.21; 12 sts. recited, then at my request he sang the first two stanzas. Learned from Jack Underwood of Blackville up on Elliot Brook, a tributary of Burnt Hill, about 35 years before. Knew it was both by and about Joe Scott, but understood the girl was from Island Falls, Maine. Compare to version dictated to Frederick Welch, July 20, 1965, NFA Ms.431.6-13.

NB.13 Mrs. Alice Flynn, Allegany, N.Y., as put together by her sisters and brothers remembering how their father, Jack McGinley of Johnville, N.B., used to sing it. Fragment of 3 sts. Given to me in Bangor, Me., August 1,1964. Knew it was by and about Joe Scott; father had known both Joe and Lizzie, she said.

NB.14 Mrs. Mabel Carr, c.60, Cantebury, N.B., July 18,1965. Written down from her recitation by Ruth Collicott, NFA 79.2. 1 1/2 sts. w/o tune. Fragment.

NB.15 Mrs. Phyllis Woodside, Milltown, N.B., sent me in a letter dated July 5,1964; fragment of 6 sts. w/o tune. Learned from her mother. Joe Scott "taught these songs to my grandmother and my mother, who was a young girl at the time. My mother sang the songs so often I learned them well."

NB.16   Joseph Pagett, 68, Markhamville, (Sussex, R.R.5), N.B., October 12, 1965; collected by E.D.I., NFA Ives tape 65.22; 7 sts. w/tune. Learned from Ora Wallace "on the drive on Big Salmon River," about 45 years before. Never knew who the author was. Believed it to be a true song which originated in Ireland. Earlier, August 31, 1964, Mr. Pagett had sent me a manuscript version, very similar to version he sang, but lacking present stanza 4. See pages 118-120 above.

NB.17   Lloyd Belyea, Brown's Flat, N.B., in a letter to me dated July 19, 1964; 13 sts. (6 d.sts. w/chorus), w/o tune. "I can't remember any other place that I heard it only from my father and he had a copy of it." Exact source of his manuscript copy is not certain.

NB.18   Spurgeon Allaby, c.70, Passekeag, N.B., in a letter to me dated July 14, 1964; fragment of 5 sts. w/o tune. Did not know who wrote it. Heard it sung by several different people but recalls specifically a man named William Cronk from St. Martins, N.B., with whom he worked in a portable sawmill around 1908.

NB.19   Wilfred Woodard. 78, St. Stephen, N.B., August 18, 1964; collected by E.D.I., NFA Ives tape 64.7; fragment of 1 st. w/tune. Had known Scott and knew this was by him.

NB.20   Wilmot MacDonald, 59, Glenwood, N.B., July 10, 1963; collected by E.D.I., ATL 3138.2; fragment of 2 sts. w/tune. Wilmot never cared enough for the song to learn it, but used to hear his sister Ann singing it.

NB.21   Bert Thorne, Jemseg, N.B., a manuscript sent to *Family Herald,* December 16, 1946; 12 sts. (6 d.sts.) w/o tune. Knew it was by Joe Scott. Had roomed with Scott at Simon Oakes', Rangeley Me., in 1901, and bought the song from him. Almost identical to the original slip. For further information, see above, p. 105.

NB.22 Walter M. Campbell, Daytona Beach, Florida, and Whitefield, N.H., in a letter to me dated December 15,1968. Fragment of 5 sts. Learned in St. Croix area between 1903 and 1910.

NS.1 Joseph Patterson, Caledonia, N.S., as recited to William Doerflinger, Summer, 1930; 11 sts. w/o tune. Same version is printed in *Shantymen and Shantyboys,* pages 248-249, except that there stanza 9 is omitted. Learned from Joe Scott at Summit Landing, Me., about 1905. See above p. 82 for further information.

NS.2 Peter Glode, Pubnico, N.S., no date given but sent in to William Doerflinger, who describes it as identical to NS.1 except for the following: "In another copy, by Peter Glode, and too exactly similar to Joe Patterson's to be worth printing here, the hint as to the author in the final stanza is quite lost, and it is an 'altar' which is to be found in the deep woods. In this version the chorus appears as a regular stanza, used only in the one place."

NS.3 John Bartlett Scarsdale, N.S., sent in to William Doerflinger in 1930-31. 5 1/2 sts. w/o tune.

NS.4 Clifford Beeler, Scarsdale, Lunenburg County, N.S., as collected by George Hirdt and sent to Robert W. Gordon, when he was writing his column for *Adventure.* Gordon Manuscript 2710, Archive of Folk Song, Library of Congress, Washington, D.C. 9 sts. w/o tune.

NS.5 MacOdrum Collection, Dahousie University Library, Halifax, Nova Scotia, pages 205-208; 11 sts. w/o tune.

NS.6 Charles W. Budge, New Haven, Victoria County, N.S., in a letter to me dated June 15,1964; 12 sts. w/o tune. Learned from a man who "in his younger days worked in the lumberwoods in Maine."

PI.1 Edmund Doucette, Miminegash, P.E.I., July 14,1963; collected by E.D.I., ATL 3153.4; 8 sts. w/tune, then added a stanza he had left out. Was not sure of all of it. Learned it locally from Fred Daigle about fifty years ago.

PI.2 John O'Connor, c.65, Hope River, P.E.I., August 31,1965; collected by E.D.I., NFA Ives tape 65.11; 11 sts. w/tune. Learned locally from a Gabe Warren about 40 years ago. See above p. 110, for further information.

PI.3 Philip Cameron, c.70, Wellington, P.E.I., August 28,1965; collected by E.D.I., NFA Ives tape 65.6; fragment of 1 1/2 sts. w/tune. Learned about 55 years ago from an uncle, Michael Cameron, who used to travel to The States to work in the woods, Cameron says he never learned the whole of it. Also had sent me a manuscript of the same fragment in a letter dated March 9,1965.

PI.4 Mrs. Underhill Coughlin, c.65, Brooklyn, P.E.I., August 23, 1965; collected by E.D.I., NFA Ives tape 65.3; fragment of 3 sts. w/tune. Learned locally.

PI.5 William J. Ballum, Summerside, P.E.I., in a letter to me dated May 22, 1959, 6 sts. w/o tune. "This may be the complete song and there may be another verse or two. It has a lovely tune to it."

BC.1 B.H. Rix, Kamloops, B.C., in a letter to the *Family Herald*, no date given but sometime in the mid-forties; 11 sts. w/o tune. See above, page 91 for further information.

BC.2 Jack A. Scott, Salmon Arm, B.C., in a letter to the *Family Herald* dated November 18,1957. He claims he made it up on a river drive in Maine in 1902. See above, pages 91-92 for further information. 12 sts. w/o tune.

APPENDIX I:

A DESCRIPTIVE LIST OF SONGS AND BALLADS WRITTEN BY JOE SCOTT OR ATTRIBUTED TO HIM

Note: This list is in no sense final or authoritative. There may be other pieces Scott wrote of which I haven't yet heard, and some of the pieces here may not be by Scott at all. For each item I give a plot summary or a description and a single stanza, usually the first. Any further versions of, or information on, any of these songs will be gratefully received and given proper credits.

BENJAMIN DEANE (LawsF-32)

Benjamin prospers in his business at Berlin Falls, but thirst for more gold leads him to selling liquor illegally and running a "free and easy house." After pleading with him to reform, his wife leaves him for another man. Deane goes to the house where she is staying and finds her there with the other man. In a fit of jealous rage he shoots her dead. From prison he warns others to avoid his fate.

> Good people all both great and small read these lines penned by me
> These   lines are written by a man deprived of liberty
> Who is serving out a sentence for a deed that I have done
> And its here I fear I will remain, 'til my race on earth is run.

(Benjamin Deane shot his wife, Berlin, N.H., May 4, 1898).

* * * * * *

THE BOOZY BOUNDARY LINE

A description of some taverns that used to stand on the boundary line between Houlton, Maine, and Woodstock, New Brunswick.

> There's a little town just down around in Aroostook County, Maine
> I've lots of times been in the town and may go back again.

* * * * * *

CHARMING LITTLE GIRL

Sometimes called "Walter Clements." A humorous song about an exceedingly ugly girl.

> Charming little girl, so pretty, neat, and sweet
> Her mouth extends from ear to ear, her chin and nose they meet.

* * * * * *

GUY REED (Laws C-9)

While breaking in a landing on the Androscoggin River, Guy is killed when the entire landing collapses and the logs crush him. He is buried "by the order of K.P." in the family plot.

> How well do I remember one dark and stormy night
> The rain it fell in torrents and the lightning flashed so bright
> The moon and stars above me, could not their light reveal
> For dark clouds so gloomy did their welcome lights conceal.

(Guy Reed was killed September 9, 1897, near Riley, Maine.)

* * * * * *

HOWARD CAREY (Laws E-23)

(The name is often given as Currie, Carrick, Kerrick, Kerwick, etc.). Howard leaves his happy New Brunswick home after his mother gives him a long lecture on the wickedness of the world. His family moves to Massachusetts and four years later he is called home to see his dying mother. He arrives too late. After that he falls into a life of wickedness. Saying that whiskey and bad women have been his undoing, he hangs himself in his room in Rumford Falls.

> My name is Howard Carey, in Grand Falls I was born
> In a pleasant little village on the banks of the St. John
> Where the small birds chant their notes so true and the
>   tumbling waters roar
> And the ivy vine does thickly twine round that cottage on
>   the shore.

(Howard Carrick hanged himself, Rumford, Maine, May 5, 1897).

* * * * * *

JACK GREEN

I know almost nothing of this piece save that a song by this title has been attributed to Scott. Sometimes the last name is omitted and the song is "about a fellow named Jack." It tells of a murder. I have only two lines (or one line!):

> Put up your weapon, Jack / Your angry passion curb,

* * * * * *

JOHN LADNER (Laws dC-40)

(This is actually *not* the ballad printed in Barry, *The Maine Woods Songster,* p. 72, but another one by the same title). John leaves his native Prince Edward Island to look for work, finally winding up in Madison, Maine. He is killed there on thanksgiving Day, when a log landing he is working on breaks and the logs crush him. His body is sent home: "a lonely grave for him does wait down on Prince Edward's Isle."

> You sympathetic friends draw near and listen to my song
> While I relate the cruel fate of a young man dead and gone
> Who now lies silent in his grave without one care or pain
> Prince Edward's Isle his native home, John Ladner by name.

(John Ladner was killed in Madison, Maine, November 29, 1900. Probably not written by Scott).

* * * * * *

THE KIND OLD PROVINCE

A man leaves New Brunswick for Maine. In Patten he meets a bartender who tells him (with tears in his eyes) how homesick he is for New Brunswick.

> I left the kind old province in the merry month of June
> The fiddleheads in blossom and the buckwheat in full bloom
> The old folks they did cry and weep the day I went away
> I went up to Fort Fairfield to help old Kinney hay.

* * * * * *

THE MAID WITH THE GOLDEN HAIR (The White Café)

A young man, looking for entertainment, walks into the White Café. He meets a beautiful girl, offers to buy her a drink, and discovers that she has an enormous capacity for liquor. She talks him into taking her to Augusta. They register at the hotel, but within the week she slips out on him, taking his money and all his possessions. The ballad ends with an account of what he will do to her when and if he finds her.

> Kind people pay attention to a few facts I would mention
> Concerning what befell me one day as I did stray
> It being on a Monday, I had been drunk on Sunday

To sober up I did stroll down to the White Café.

* * * * * *

NORMAN MITCHELL (The Patten Maid)

Brought up in Patten, Maine, Mitchell marries a beautiful girl in spite of warnings that she is false. She gets bolder and bolder in her stepping out on him, and finally one day someone sends him a photograph of his wife in the nude as proof of her perfidy. Mitchell drinks poison and falls dead at his wife's feet.

(Norman Mitchell committed suicide March 14,1909).

* * * * * *

THE NORWAY BUM

An old bum tells his story, saying he is a man who "has seen better days." As a young man he fell in love with a girl whom his family felt was beneath him, and when he married her they disinherited him. However, he settled in Norway and set up a medical practice there. One night he was returning from seeing a patient and heard the firebell ringing: "Norway was fast burning down." He found his own house in flames and saw his wife and child screaming for help from an upstairs window, but no-one could save them and they fell back in the flames and perished. He ends the song by saying that in order to drown his sorrow he took to drinking rum.

> Do you think by my dress I would rob a hen's nest
> Or do anything that was bad
> If you think that I would I will tell you the truth
> You would strike the nail fair on the head.

(Poem first appeared in print in *Rumford Falls Times,* April 13, 1901).

* * * * * *

THE PLAIN GOLDEN BAND (Laws H-17)

A Young man (or not so young) recalls his parting from Lizzie, the girl he adored. She gave him back his ring, saying that she put "a stain on that plain golden band," when she met a young man who offered his love and told her false stories about her fiance. He ends the ballad by saying his love will remain pure and that they will find him "in the green shady forest so far far away."

> I am thinking tonight of the days that are gone
> When the sun clambers over the mountains at morn
> And the dewdrops from heaven like diamonds did glow
> They were kissing the rose in the valley below.

* * * * * *

REST GENTLE ROSE

This piece has been reported only in the following fragment:

> Rest gentle Rose in death's calm repose
> Rest while the wind makes the wild willows wave
> Wild roses bloom o'er her early tomb
> She sleeps in the flowery vale.

* * * * * *

SACKER SHEEHAN'S LITTLE GIRL

The girl tells her story. Her father is a drunkard, her mother dead. She wanders into the town one cold and stormy night and stands forlornly outside a gay ballroom. A fine lady picks her up and takes her home with her to stay

> Now I am only Sacker Sheehan's poor little girl, you know
> Who was cast upon this cruel world, no home, no place to go.

My father is a drunkard; my mother, don't you know?
Oh she left me in my infancy; she died long years ago.

* * * * * *

WHITE AND MURPHY

Wilfred White and John Murphy are drowned while trying to swim some horses across the Magalloway River on their way into the lumberwoods.

> *(Not the first stanza)*
> Now at the crossing place the river runs both deep and wide
> The ferry boat you see was lying on the northeast side
> When they would reach the southwest side there they would
>   have to wait
> Till Win York brought the boat across, who was twenty
>   minutes late.

(The accident occurred October 13, 1901).

* * * * * *

WILLIAM McGIVNEY (McGIBBENY)

A dying man looks at mementoes of his family. His first daughter died and lies buried at Anson (Me.). His wife left him, taking with her the second daughter, whom he fears will become a "woman of ill fame" like her mother. He asks that the mementoes (letters, pictures, and a lock of hair) be buried with him, and when this request is granted he dies.

> Within a cheerless cot, in a lone and desolate spot
> Lay a dying man just e'er the close of day,
> Who e'er the morning light would disperse the gloom of night
> From this world of woe and care would pass away.

* * * * * *

WILLIAM SULLIVAN

Sullivan decides to go to work in the woods in Maine and leave his New Brunswick home, though his mother pleads with him not to go, telling him of his brothers who have already left and been killed. Near Bemis he is killed when he cuts off the stump of an uprooted tree and it falls back and buries him. His body is sent back home.

> *(Not the first stanza)*
> How well do I remember, it seems but yesterday,
> Though three long and dreary years has passed since Douglas went away
> He never returned in life agin, with quivering lips she said
> They brought your brother back to me, my son but he was dead.

(Sullivan was killed October 20, 1897, near Bemis, Maine).

* * * * * *

THE WRECK ON THE GRAND TRUNK

A wreck took place on the Grand Trunk Railroad between Bethel and Locke's Mills, Maine. Two double-headed freight trains collide and one of them is carrying explosives. A number of men in the crews of both trains are killed. There is also a verse that tells of "two tramps were riding on that train that never will go tramp again."

> You bold sons of freedom your attention I'll command
> And you I will not long detain
> Of what I'm going to write, it happened in this state
> Here in this Pine Tree State of Maine.

(Date of the wreck, January 17, 1901).

* * * * * *

APPENDIX II:

Number of versions of Scott's songs Collected as of October 1, 1969. (Note: Number given *includes* fragments. Number of fragments is given in parentheses).

itle	Maine	N.B.	P.E.I.	N.S.	N.H.	Other	Total	With Tunes
enjamin Deane	8(3f)	7(4f)	2	5(3f)	3(1f)	1	26	12
oozy Boundary	(1f)	(1f)					2	
harming Little irl	1	1	(1f)				3	
uy Reed	16(3f)	17(2f)	4(2f)	3(1f)	5(1f)	2	47	24
oward Carey	9(7f)	20(8f)	8(3f)	5(2f)	1	2	45	29
hn Ladner	(2f)	1	5	1	1		10	7
ind Old Province						1	1	
aid With olden Hair	2(1f)	4					6	3
orman Mitchell	1						1	
orway Bum	9(2f)	6(1f)	6(3f)	1	1	1	24	12
ain Golden Band	16(5f)	22(7f)	5(4f)	6	2(1f)	3	54	21
est Gentle Rose		(1f)					1	
acker Sheehan's ittle Girl		1					1	

continued

Title	Maine	N.B.	P.E.I.	N.S.	N.H.	Other	Total	With Tune
White & Murphy	1				1	1(Ont. via Me.)	3	
William McGivney		1					1	
William Sullivan	1						1	
Wreck on the Grand Trunk	1	1					2	1
Totals	68	83	31	21	14	11	228	109

NOTES

[1] This present paper is part of a much longer work still in preparation: a full biography of Joe Scott and a complete study of each of his songs. Much of the material was gathered over a period of twelve years with generous help from the Coe Research Fund Committee of the University of Maine. During the academic year 1965-66 I was the recipient of a fellowship from the John Simon Guggenheim Memorial Foundation and was thus able to devote full time to the work. I would like to express my gratitude to both of these benefactors.

Throughout this paper, an asterisk before a quotation means that it is taken verbatim from a tape recorded interview.

[2] Austin: University of Texas Press, 1958.

[3] Unpublished doctoral dissertation, University of Pennsylvania, 1965. University Microfilms No. 66-4654. For another example, see Roger D. Abrahams' "Creativity, Individuality, and the Traditional Singer," in *Studies in the Literary Imagination,* Volume III, No.1, April, 1970, pages 1-34.

[4] See Ellen Stekert's article, "The Hidden Informant," *Midwest Folklore,* 13 (1963), 21-28, for an example of this kind of study.

[5] See my book, *Larry Gorman: The Man Who Made the Songs.* Bloomington, 1964).

[6] For an excellent discussion of creativity in folksong, see Stekert, *Two Voices,* pages 6-22 (her second chapter: "The Traditional Singer as a Creative Individual"). See also John Quincy Wolf, "Folksingers and the Re-Creation of Folksong," *Western Folklore,* 26(1967), 101-111; and Abrahams' work cited above.

[7] *Larry Gorman,* pages xi-xii. See also D.K. Wilgus, *Anglo-American Folksong Scholarship Since 1898* (New Brunswick, N.J., 1959), pages 289-295.

[8] For a good version of this ballad, see "Twenty-One Folksongs from Prince Edward Island," *Northeast Folklore,* V(1963), 13-17.

[9] For published versions of this ballad, see my article, "'Ben Deane' and Joe Scott: A Ballad and its Probable Author," *Journal of American Folklore,* 72(1959), 62.

[10] David C. Smith's unpublished doctoral dissertation, "A History of Lumbering in Maine 1860-1930," (Cornell, 1965), gives an excellent picture of this period and these migrations, even to examples of handbills that were distributed in the Maritimes to lure men to Maine.

[11] For eastern versions of "The Banks of the Little Eau Pleine," see *Northeast Folklore* V (1963), 48-52, and the notes on page 78.

[12] For a copy of the newspaper article, see my article, "'Ben Deane' and Joe Scott," p. 56.

[13] T.S.Eliot, "Tradition and the Individual Talent," in *Selected Essays 1917-1932* (New York, 1932), page 4.

[14] Phillips Barry, "Communal Re-creation," *Bulletin of the Folk-Song Society of the Northeast,* Number 5 (1933), 5.

[15] For various statements of this concept, see Gordon Hall Gerould, *The Ballad of Tradition* (Oxford, 1932) pages 163-188.

[16] Manuscript sent to me by Mr. Doerflinger, February 27, 1966.

[17] For further data, see notes in the Appendix under NB.1. Here, as again on page 118 the transcription has been transposed so that G is the final. The original key and opening pitches are given in a catch-signature at the end of the tune.

[18] Gordon Manuscript 2710.

[19] Letter to the author dated September 11, 1957.

[20] *Journal of American Folklore,* 64 (1951), 437.

[21] Letter to the author dated March 5, 1957.

[22] I would like to take this opportunity to thank Bill Perkins who was Rumford's Town Clerk during the time I was searching the records there in the mid sixties. His interest and assistance—and that of his staff—made my work there not only rewarding but pleasant.

[23] For a good description of the development of Rumford, see Smith,

"History of Lumbering in Maine," page 446 *et. seq.* See also State of Maine, Bureau of Industrial and Labor Statistics, *Sixteenth Annual Report, 1902,* pages 116-154, "The Development of Rumford Falls."

[24] *Rumford Falls Times,* April 5, 1895.

[25] See, for example, "The Old Elm Tree" in Phillips Barry, *The Maine Woods Songster* (Cambridge, Mass., 1939), p. 34.

[26] For easily available versions of the tune to "Bendemeer's Steam," see William Cole, *Folk Songs of England, Ireland, Scotland, and Wales* (Garden City, N.Y., 1961), pages 78-79, or Margaret Bradford Boni, *The Fireside Book of Folk Songs* (New York, 1947), pages 20-21.

[27] For "Slavery Days," see "Folksongs from Maine," *Northeast Folklore,* VII (1965), 45-48.

[28] Franz Rickaby, *Ballads and Songs of the Shantyboy* (Cambridge, Mass., 1926), page 26.

[29] Manus O'Conor, Irish *Com-All-Ye's* (New York, 1901), page 80.

[30] See above, page 98.

[31] In a letter to me dated June 15, 1964 in which he sent me version NS.6.

[32] In a letter to me dated June 21, 1964, in which he sent me version NB.4.

[33] See version NB.16. For further discussion of singers' belief that songs are "true," see Herbert Halpert's Introductory Essay, "Truth in Folk-Songs— Some Observations on the Folk-Singer's Attitude," in John Harrington Cox, *Traditional Ballads and Folk-Songs Mainly from West Virginia* (Philadelphia, 1964), pages xiii-xx.

[34] *The Family Herald,* November 19, 1895. I would like to take this opportunity to thank the following members of the staff of this newspaper for making the "Old Favourites" files available to me while I was in Montreal in January, 1966: Vernon Pope, Senior Advisory Editor; Peter Hendry, Editor; C.M. Lapointe, Librarian; and particularly Sheila Bucher, Assistant Fiction Editor and at that time running the "Old Favourites" section.

[35] See above, p. 88.

[36] See NB.16 given in full above on pages 118-120.

[37] Fannie Hardy Eckstorm and Mary Winslow Smyth, *Minstrelsy of Maine* (Boston and New York, 1927), p. 36.

[38] See, for example, Jim Brown's version given above on pages 87-89.

[39] Me.15 and NB.14.

[40] See footnote 17.

[41] See above, page 112.

[42] James Reginald Wilson, "Ballad Tunes of the Miramichi," unpublished Master's Thesis, New York University, 1961, page 25. For a study of some of the permutations of the "Villikins" tune, see Phillips Barry, "Notes on the Ways of Folk-Singers with Folk-Tunes," *Bulletin of the Folk-Song Society of the Northeast*, Number 12, (1937), 2-6.

[43] See above, page 98.

[44] For examples of this phenomenon, compare "The Boys of the Island" as it is found in Doerflinger, page 218, with the same song as it appears in *Larry Gorman*, pages 123-124. See also "The Old Elm Tree" as it was reported by Barry in the *Journal of American Folklore*, 27 (1914), 69-70, and that song as it appears in the same author's *Maine Woods Songster*, page 34.

[45] For W.N. (Billy) Allen, see Rickaby, pages xxix-xxxviii and elsewhere *passim*. For Orville Jenks, see George Korson, *Coal Dust on the Fiddle* (Hatboro, Pa., 1965), page 447-448, and elsewhere *passim*. For John Calhoun, see Louise Manny, "The Ballad of Peter Amberley," *The Atlantic Advocate*, 53 (July 1963), 67-74. For N. Howard ("Jack")Thorp, see his *Songs of the Cowboys*, edited by Austin E. and Alta S. Fife (New York, 1966), and also John O. West, "Jack Thorp and John Lomax: Oral or Written Transmission?" *Western Folklore*, 26 (1967), 113-118. For the Rev. Andrew Jenkins, there is a brief account in D.K. Wilgus' article, "The Rationalistic Approach," in *A Good Tale and a Bonnie Tune*, Publication of the Texas Folklore Society XXXII (1964), pages 227-237. To this list should be added two studies by Loman Cansler: "Walter Dibben, An Ozark Bard," *Kentucky Folklore Record*, XIII (1967), and "He Hewed His Own Path: William Henry Scott, Ozark Songmaker," in *Studies in the Literary Imagination*, Volume III, Number 1 (April, 1970), published by Georgia State Univ., Atlanta, Ga., pages 37-63.

PAUL E. HALL:
A NEWFOUNDLAND SONG-MAKER
AND HIS COMMUNITY OF SONG

BY

JOHN F. SZWED

Paul E. Hall

Paul E. Hall:
A Newfoundland Song-Maker
And His Community Of Song[1]

by

John F. Szwed

Anyone sampling the literature of folksong must find it difficult not to be impressed by the range and depth of the scholarship. There is simply no area of folkloristic learning to match it. The knowledge of folksong poetics is such that we are satisfied to put song alongside other forms of literature; we have distributional studies that give us a basis for talking about song across time and space; we know a great deal about the norms of song, so that we can even talk of cliches and deviations from traditional patterns; and more recently we have begun to develop the tools to deal with such elusive matter as melody and singing style. Yet there is one area of folksong scholarship that is a blank: it remains for us to discover what the songs mean to their singers and their listeners.

It is to this problem and its solution in the ethnographic reality of song that this essay is addressed. Through a brief portrait

of a Newfoundland folksong artist and one of his songs I hope to
show how much we need to know, and how much remains available to
us in the lives and songs of folk creators.

I

If we are to understand folksongs, if we are to make sense
of their use by a people, there must be a concerted effort to discover
the ethnographic reality of song: that is, we must try to understand
the native conception of reality that lies behind a song, motivates it,
and relates the verbal content of the song to the content of other areas
of a culture.[2] The question to be asked here is not overly difficult:
what is it about a song that leads one person to repeat it to another
once the song has been created and presented within a specific context?
We have to explain the movement of musical behavior from a momentary,
situational expediency to a new status as normative or "traditional."

The singing of songs must, in some manner or other, relate to
the unfolding drama that is the human community. Traditional songs
--like the community and its institutions--outlive the individual actors
involved, so for them to persist through time they must speak to
individuals in terms of cultural constants. The folklorists' particular
preoccupation with processes of transmission (and the overworked
oral-written dichotomy) has ignored the more basic question of the
social basis of persistence of given forms of communication. The
locus of the continuity of folklore forms may finally be found in the
social roles of a community (its "table of personnel") and their relation
to the persistent problems of community organization and survival.

A folksong may be thought of as one of many means by which
man adapts to his natural and social environments over time; that is,
as one of many means by which life chances are maximized through
a human design. If the song is effective again and again in the adaptational process, and not just a temporary situational solution, it
will have survival value. Even though the purpose of a given song may
be one of short-term expediency, appealing only to given individuals,
if it shows itself to have broader-reaching value as well, it can move
into the realm of the normative (i.e., into the category of societal values,

where its persistence becomes a matter of broader sanction than that of individual choice). In other words, the results of a summation of individual aesthetic-ethical choices become prescribed behavior.

We may also think of songs as reflecting various selective pressures that operate unevenly, and ultimately derive from the nature of given problems in the community's social and natural existence. For example, we might expect persisting songs to be those that relate to questions of social conflict and solidarity within the total community unit.

Although these very brief remarks on theoretical aspects of folksong are painfully general, it should at least be apparent that the failure of folksong scholars to examine the social meaning of song is very serious. The reasons for this failure are not difficult to discover. In large part, it reflects an overemphasis and misunderstanding of the processes of cultural continuity and change that derive from nineteenth century evolutionary theory and its explanations of cultural survivals. In turn, this misplaced emphasis results, first, in an overconcern with ballads at the cost of other folksongs because of their relative age, formality, and wide distribution, and second, in an attitude that finds fieldwork of secondary importance, if not irrelevant. Part of the problem, too, is that anthropology--so often the source of folklore theory--has itself failed to provide the guidance equal to that offered in studies of mythology. In the process of encountering the heavily redundant songs of hunting and gathering and tribal peoples, anthropologists simply did not seek ethnographic detail in song as they did in myth.

But for whatever reasons, folklorists' failures have left them facing a curious irony: Western folksong contains some of the least redundant and most information-laden texts[3] in the world, and yet these texts have gone without serious attempts to understand their meaning in social context. Western folksingers go to great pains to make their messages clear and interesting, often uninterrupted by accompaniment, audience participation or comment: the least we can do is to try and understand what it is they are trying to communicate.

II

I first met Paul E. Hall on the steep trail to his house atop a hill that overlooks the Gulf of St. Lawrence on the western coast of Newfoundland. Paulie stepped out from behind a bush, and, in the manner of Newfoundlanders, began a conversation as though we were old friends: "I was just out to see the sights," he said, gesturing towards the Gulf, where the coming darkness revealed the flickering lights of fishing boats twenty or thirty miles out. With hardly a pause, he went on to talk of ghost ships, sailing disasters, Nazi U-boats, the Joe Louis-Max Baer fight, moose, and politics from 1920 to 1930. As Alan Lomax once wrote of folk singer Estil Ball of Rugby, Va., it was as though he had been preparing for my visit for decades.

In Paulie's house--a one-room, unpainted hut, braced against the cyclonic winds of Southwestern Newfoundland--I heard an oral autobiography as carefully fashioned as a bard's epic. Born on November 9, 1897, Hall spent his life in the fishing-farming-logging and occasional wage-labor pattern common to the people of his home area, the Codroy Valley. Here, he grew up among the scattering of Roman Catholic Irish, English, Scots, French, and Indian settlers who came to the 100 square miles of the Codroy Valley in the early nineteenth century. Like other young men of the Valley, he tested the outside world when he was in his teens, first in the logging camps, then, in the spring, aboard the sealing ships. But after a few years, he joined the small group of boys who in every generation choose to stay home and continue subsistence farming rather than to go to Nova Scotia, Toronto, or Boston.

The people of the Codroy Valley are fiercely independent, self-reliant, and egalitarian.[4] Like peasants in many parts of the world, they are at the mercy of an inconsistent market; so income is at best a mysterious, unpredictable factor that again and again drives a man back to his home soil where traditional crops and home-made goods are stable. In such a society land is almost sacred, and the use of it an obligation. But at the same time the goods of the world are viewed statically, suspiciously, and competition is frowned upon: those who attempt to rise economically or socially, who become "high and mighty," are held in contempt. Leadership and external control are minimized, and each man sees it as his duty to keep the peace and to maintain traditional order.

This is the life that Paulie Hall accepted at age 17, having a good idea of what he had lost and what he was gaining by staying on the "homestead." But his life took a different turn from that of most of his neighbors. He continued to live with his parents--his father, an "awful pleasant man, a comical man but with no backbone and lazy," his mother, a hard-working, durable woman--until he was 38. For reasons known only to Paulie he never married; so he built "some kind of a shelter" across the road and up the hill from his parent's home, where he still remains, several miles from the nearest neighbor. Without the family help needed to maintain a subsistence farm, he soon gave up most crops and settled on cutting cord wood for sale to distant paper mills.

Today Paulie's house is cramped with an accumulation of a lifetime; bottles of home-brew, an assortment of farm and woods tools, hand-carved butter paddles, hats, calendars, and buckets fill the tiny space. An assortment of socks have been drying over the stove for the four years I have known him and, for all I know, have been dry for twenty years. Most striking, though, is an astonishing pile of newspapers and magazines dating back to the 1920's; one pile, covered with a sheepskin, forms a day-bed. Having had no formal education, Paulie as a young man set out to become a reader:

> I didn't know the letters in the book when I came to live by myself, but now I can pick up a book or paper and crack it off with the average, and if I comes to a word I can't pronounce, well, I'll spell it out, pick the syllables out of it. . .a good start on a word you can't read. I learned most letters, but in the small alphabet, the p's and the q's, the b's and the d's, the m's and the w's, sometimes I used to get mixed up. By and by I came to look at a book and read the heading and I knewed what was there and I started in to read just the same as if I knew what was coming.

His reading skill is a point of pride, and he surrounds himself with literature of various kinds, all of which he keeps on hand "just in case I need'em in a dispute."

> One time I did throw some of 'em away. . .
> I put 'em outside and a bad storm come up
> and blowed some of 'em against the window,
> about to break it. "By God," I said, "you was
> my friends and now you've turned on me!"

The solitary life of the bachelor led Hall to seek other forms of self-amusement. When he was in his 40's he made his first song, "something to do while I was hauling in wood with my mare." Unable to write the words down, he made them in "bachelor's style."

> It was like a machine. . .I had to sing it and keep
> it coming fast or I couldn't get it to stay in me
> mind. I don't know how you would describe it.
> If I set me mind to make a song, the rest come just
> the same as an endless chain--I could just make
> the verse and sing it, just keep going. If I made a
> verse and got stuck a little bit, I just might have to
> sing that verse over five or six times, but I'd just
> continue and sing. If it didn't sound right, well,
> I'd go back and change words till I would get it
> right. Then, when I'd made my songs coming
> over the hill hauling wood, I'd come in the
> house that night, there was no one around, and
> I'd sing that five or six times. . .I had a good
> memory. . .it stayed right there, and I'd sing it often,
> probably three or four times a day until I had it
> right off, by heart, before I'd tackle another one.

This is the process that Paulie sees as a "gift," the same kind of gift that marked him as a good teller of jokes in the community. Both he sees as part of a continuum, as his songs are sung jokes, humorous insights into the people he knew. "Serious songs"--the classic tragic ballads--he saw as morbid, and never cared for them.

But if Paul was a poet, he was not a musician, choosing to borrow melodies:

> I'd just start in and make the verse and sing
> it, put an air to it. . .probably I'd use two or
> three airs to see which one would suit the best,
> 'till I'd get one that I'd kind of like myself. . .
> I'd build on that one.

This composition process is most common to the Northeastern part of North America and many parts of the world where the text and its story-telling qualities are dominant in the song performance. It is not surprising, then, to discover that most of Hall's songs have melodies drawn from traditional folksongs and older popular ditties.

Paulie says that his first songs were songs "on himself," for he felt that it was better to test his abilities on his audience in as safe a way as possible. After his first successes he moved on to more daring efforts, and settled into the central tradition of Northeastern song-making: satire and sarcasm. Although he insists that all of his songs were just "in fun," Hall admitted that some did not take his songs as such, and on more than one occasion he was threatened to cease his efforts.

> When they found out I could make a good song,
> some of the young fellas would come around
> and give me the pointers about people so that I
> could make one. . .but then sometimes I'd turn
> it around and made one on them that gave me the
> facts, so that they'd be more careful the next
> time.

Some of his songs were so intensely embarrassing to the whole community and its sense of propriety that when they were sung again by others, one or another stanza was abandoned. In Paulie's song about unorthodox courting procedures (*Winnie McNeil*), the key figure—George—is alternatively made a sniveling suitor and a sly rake:

> The time it has come now at least, I might say,
> For us to appoint our wedding day;
> I think we'll appoint it down in John Dan's hay;
> I don't mean the hay that's around in the field,
> Oh Winnie, oh Winnie, oh Winnie McNeil.

This clandestine meeting in a nearby farmer's barn was dropped in later versions of the song. Although the song was Paulie's, the community remade it to their taste--not a surprising occurrence from what we know of folksong transmission.

The fact is that the degree of social invective and abuse found in the local satirical songs of the Northeast makes them difficult for the outsider to collect, and they are conspicuously absent from a number of area collections. As William Doerflinger suggests, such songs are gossip in its most malignant form.[5] Like gossip, satirical songs are a private view of affairs of public interest, loaded with special pleading. Unlike gossip, on the other hand, they make public a private assessment of a situation in the candid manner that only song can do. The satirical songmaker walks the thin line between amusement and libel.

As I've suggested, the satirical songs of the Codroy Valley are similar to those found throughout Newfoundland and the rest of the eastern part of the North American continent.[6] Although this genre awaits further subdivision and definition, it is clear that it includes songs commemorating names and minor incidents, boasts of unorthodox personal achievements, and intense social criticism of others.[7] Paul's own creations, for example, are exclusively devoted to satirical characterization and parody; his plots are thin, and indeed, he thinks of events as being unimportant. For his songs, the "pointers" are only means of launching personal appraisals of individuals' behavior.

Even though the Valley's songs of satire do not deal with major incidents, they nevertheless treat matters of local consequence: the oppressive tactics of game wardens, the objectionable behavior of entrepreneurs, fights, thefts, and problems of work and love. Such songs are tools of social control, and their makers potential agents of public censure. Yet even though they are community spokesmen, song-makers are viewed with ambivalent feelings. Like the famous Maine woods poet Larry Gorman, no one is ever really safe from their gifts of wit.[8] From what little we know of song-makers elsewhere, Paulie Hall is typical in being seen as an eccentric and in being held somewhat apart from the community around him. He is "a character...a case...a strange one."

Paulie's view of himself is complementary to that of his community. He sees his talent as singular. Like the jazz innovator Jelly Roll Morton or the gifted Trinidadian folk violinist Vivian Moses, he feels that his skill and accomplishment have been wasted on his listeners, and he longs to reach a larger audience. It was not surprising to him that I should be interested in his singing, for he thinks his songs are valuable and should reach a more appreciative public, though ironically, the thrust of his songs is so localized as to make them virtually meaningless to those outside of a few farm communities. Paul sees himself as an artist in exile among his own people.

The Bachelor's Song

1. There is a house upon a hill;
   It is a bachelor's hall.
   And the bachelor who lives in it,
   His name is Paulie Hall.

　　　　　Refrain

　　To my tippie-tippie, tip-top, tip-top,
　　tip-top, tippie-tippie, tip-top day.

2.　And now as I will tell you
　　I am living at my ease.
　　I go out just when I'm ready
　　And come in just when I please.

　　　　　Refrain

3.　I does all my own cooking
　　And I wash and mend my clothes;
　　Sure, and every second Friday,
　　Oh, I polish up my stove.

　　　　　Refrain

4.　I does all my own out-door work
　　And milk and get my wood;
　　And I does it with a right good will,
　　As a good old bachelor should.

　　　　　Refrain

5.　I have no wife to bother me
　　For to spend on paint or rouge;
　　So you see I have some extra
　　When I want to have a booze.

　　　　　Refrain

6.　Just now you might imagine
　　What she'd spend to buy a puff;
　　If you had it in a beer shop
　　It would get you beer enough.

Refrain

7. When a month's work it is ended
   After a mighty hard drag;
   I'll step out some fine evening
   And take on a great big jag.

   Refrain

8. Next morning when I get up
   My head is mighty bad;
   And I hear a woman scolding
   And you bet I feel some glad.

   Refrain

9. Now if I had a woman
   You would hear her scold and damn.
   By the look upon her cross face
   She was eating sour jam.

   Refrain

10. Now some fine spring in the June month
    When my last seed it is growed,
    And there's not one tree left standing
    On my farm, below the road.

    Refrain

11. When all this work is ended
    That I have planned in my mind,
    I'll go searching through this world
    'Till a partner, I will find.

    Refrain

12. I can't get a wife around here:
    You all know how hard I looked.
    So I'll join the train at Doyles,
    And I'll go to Journois Brook.

    Refrain

13. And for a dame at Journois Brook
    I'm going to take a hen.
    Oh, as soon as I arrive there
    It's courting I'll begin.

    Refrain

14. With a hen under my coat,
    Sir, don't you wish me luck;
    And in my breeches pocket
    Go a stick of old black duck.

    Refrain

15. And when I get up to Journois Brook
    In order for to win,
    I will give my coat a little shake,
    And out will pop my hen.

    Refrain

16. I'll stay around at Journois Brook
    For one week and a day;
    Then I'll tighten up my collar
    And I'll go on to Flat Bay.

    Refrain

17. I'll stay around at Flat Bay
     Till all the girls are grown;
     And I'll tighten up my collar
     And I'll go to Shallop's Cove.

     Refrain

18. I'll stay around at Shallop's Cove
     Till it's "no," the girls all said;
     And once more I'll cut my whiskers off
     And try around Bank Head.

     Refrain

19. I won't stay long at Bank Head;
     My heart will be so sore.
     Oh, I'll say the hell with the hen and girls,
     I'll go to the Labrador.

     Refrain

20. And every little Husky girl
     That I see, far or near,
     I will pop the question to her:
     "Will you marry me, my dear?"

     Refrain

The *Bachelor's Song* is a song in local circulation in the Codroy Valley, and was made by Paul E. Hall in the 1930's. Such a satirical song presents an especially interesting problem in the study of continuity. For such songs to survive beyond the lives of the original personalities and beyond the incidents recounted they must contain more than the initial elements of personalized satire. Time can quickly dull a song that once cut deeply with the keenest of sardonic devices. In fact, it may be difficult for the outsider to understand even the original point of such a song. But we are not so hampered when we seek to understand why a song appeals to a community beyond its original set of historical and temporal referents.

The Bachelor's Song unquestionably refers to Paul Hall himself. The song is Paul's and he first sang it himself, although he gave it no name. However, the implications of the title[9] are important, and the title the community gave it leads us to ask about the role of the bachelor.

Bachelorhood in many societies is a potentially disruptive status (at least in those societies where marriage implies manhood): the bachelor rests in an uneasy category filled with some of both boy's and man's characteristics. In partilineal and partilocal societies, such as those of much of Newfoundland, the importance of land and associated family activities makes an unmarried adult male a more problematic category than that of an unmarried adult female. Speaking of a small community of the northeast coast of Newfoundland, James Faris says "unmarried men are not whole in a very real way...," and "there are few structural options for the unmarried adult."[10]

But perhaps a more useful way of seeing the bachelor's position in Newfoundland peasant society is to briefly consider the fact that peasant communities frequently conceive of resources as being limited and fixed in their relationship to the community;[11] within such a conception one person's success is often seen to be at the expense of everyone else. Also in such a negative framework there is often a tendency towards bickering, negative gossip, and back-biting, such as has been described for parts of Mexico, Italy and elsewhere.[12] But the notion of a static economy does not necessarily rule out all cooperation. Inter-familial mutual assistance without petty bickering does occur, for example, within the conception of limited good in parts of Ireland and Newfoundland, where social control is particularly rooted in the activities which affect the allocation of scarce resources.[13] In the Codroy Valley such activities are those connected with sexual behavior in general, and marital and family alignment in particular. In the Valley a tendency towards age-grading, norms of pre-marital chastity, a pattern of land access and birth control through delayed marriage, and exogamous marriage at the village level, all suggest that the scarce resources of farmland, pasture, woodland, water, and the traditional activities that control them are all subject to careful scrutiny and a resulting degree of tension.

In such a setting, the bachelor holds a position that is simultaneously seen as pitiful and threatening. On one hand, he is socially incomplete, unable to fully participate in the usual pattern of reciprocity that involves food and farm labor (such as a wife and children can provide), and on the other, he is a source of potential disorder, lacking sons that bring continuity of land and solidarity of community territoriality. In the same manner, the bachelor's lack of legitimate sexual outlets is a source for community concern. The potentiality for sexual disruptance is most effectively seen in the fact that a number of drunken bachelors often flamboyantly step-dance in front of married women at community parties. Tension is also revealed in the joking done by married men at the expense of the bachelor.

Bachelorhood in the Valley is only acceptable if the bachelor has tried to marry and has failed: the choice not to marry is not socially approved. In the same way, childless marriages and the marriage of persons after the age of child-bearing is frowned upon, and often results in severe ostracism. All of these concerns have been accentuated since the 1930's, as economic changes have resulted in a greater number of resident bachelors. An old problem has been newly intensified.

As peripheral as such ethnographic details may seem, it is only in light of such information that we can understand the community's affinity for *The Bachelor's Song*.

Hall's song seems almost perfectly divided into two parts: the first half (stanzas 1-9) stresses the independence of the bachelor and the manner in which he absorbs the work of women and children into that of the male's. The emphasis here is on the rigorous life of the bachelor as contrasted to that of the married man. There is a tone of pride in stanzas 5-6, where flexibility of resources is emphasized. In everyday affairs the point is evident in reciprocal "treating" behavior in local beer shops, where bachelors are able to "out-treat" their married friends, thus off-setting the married man's advantage in having a wife's food preparation for home treating-reciprocity. Stanzas 7-9 further emphasize the relative independence of the single man.

In the second portion of the song (stanzas 10-20) a curious shift occurs: the bachelor begins to explain his failures in seeking a wife (stanzas 11-12) and expresses his plans to continue his search beyond the parish (a logical extension of the principle of exogamy at the village level, as practiced by the Valley's people). From stanza 12 on, the bachelor begins his odyssey north along the Newfoundland coast. Significantly, he passes over Protestant villages, not acceptable sources of wife or doxy, in fact or fantasy. He stops at Journois Brook, Shallop's Cove, and Bank Head, settlements known on the West Coast of Newfoundland as the homes of the "Jack-o-Tars," or "dark people"–the French-Indians. Although Catholic, the people of these areas are viewed by Valley people as immoral, destitute, and as an extreme of cultural deviancy. Paul Hall remarked on this portion of his song:

> Well, you know that was a place! They seemed to be awfully rough people in Journois Brook. Well, in other words, by the way of what I saw from Journois Brook, there was a whole lot there wasn't very respectable people and this is why I made it. You know I made this as bad as I could. God, they were hard cases there, boy. My God, well, it was inhuman. No person could even laugh at it even, it was too. . .it was outright brutish, straight through, nine out of ten I run up against.

But Paul could laugh at it, and so do all the singers and listeners who enjoy the song, as Hall himself admits:

> Well, now there was a joke. . .most people here knew it. . .you go in there with a

> plug of tobacco or a hen and you could
> go and sleep with any woman in Journois
> Brook.

The *double entendre* of hens and ducks thus has a basis in local economics.

The bachelor's failure to achieve feminine companionship even at the extremes of his own culture—at the point of pathology—pushes him to travel on to the northern edge of the hemisphere, outside of his cultural realm: to look for a mate among the Eskimo is an act of such desperation as to be thought the height of absurdity.

This curious song is for Valley people the most amusing one they know. Yet the humor exists because of the community's ambivalence towards bachelorhood, as reflected in the song's two opposed sections. The bachelor is independent, but at the cost of being socially incomplete. He is in a state that can be tolerated only if all avenues of escape have been exhausted. By his statement that he no longer has any possibilities left within his own community he renders himself harmless by showing that he would seek sexual outlet only at the peripheries or outside of his culture. Yet, significantly, he would attempt this only after making proper use of the homestead he has inherited (stanzas 10-11). The song seems to say that, after exhausting his farm's natural resources, he is free to try and exhaust his own, but far away from the community.

In Paulie Hall's old age and failing health, he is seldom seen by more than a few members of his community. Many people now know who he is only by the song that lives in his absence, and speaks for his condition and for those who share his plight. When young people ask to hear "that old Bachelor's song" they respond to a humorous comment on a social problem that remains a source of anxiety and tension in their community.

My approach to understanding the song's meaning certainly does not exhaust the possibilities: *The Bachelor's Song* may have even more private meanings in relation to Hall's life or to those who are bachelors in the community. Certainly it has certain similarities to songs such as Larry Gorman's *Bachelor's Hall*,[14] with its numerous allusions that beg for psychoanalytic interpretation. Yet it is only by direct reference to the ethnographic facts of its community that one can begin to understand its meaning to local people and its persistence beyond Hall's own singing.

It is worth noting that an interpretation such as this does not depend on there being a perfect reflection of cultural facts within the song's text: bachelors' quests for mates are rare, and certainly Eskimo women are out of the question. If folklore were simply a matter of "mirror-image" statements of a culture, then ethnography could be replaced by folklore collection. But where we do not expect to find direct embodiments of cultural data in folklore items, it is not surprising to discover social structural problems accurately mirrored by such material. It may be that the irreducible minimum in folklore is social structure, where the roles and statuses of a community are restated in one or another form as a basis for comment, whether humorous, tragic or ironic. The community, after all, is the setting in which a song emerges, in which it is performed, and in which its meaning unfolds.

III

Paul Hall is, for all purposes, no longer a real part of his community. Aging and sickly, he stays close to his house, visited only by one or two neighbors and a close relative who tends to many of his needs. Once a week he descends the path and walks to the nearest shop for a few groceries and the mail. His neighbors say that he has been "failing" and that he no longer is as "smart" as he once was. Recently, he saw his first television show, as TV is the latest evidence of Canada's increasing impact on isolated Newfoundland. Paulie, like most adults in his community, finds television only mildly interesting. Coming late to the developed conventions of TV, the people of the Codroy Valley often find the programming dull, the advertisements outlandish. Paulie himself understands television to be a personal medium, and he feels that each program that he sees has been performed especially for him. From his perspective he is grateful for shows that he finds "nice and friendly;" others--such as dramas of crime and sex--disturb and embarrass him.

But television musical programs, like those of radio, have been a boon for Paulie, who enjoys music of all types. He talks glowingly of the pleasant melodies of what he calls the "short songs"--short, as opposed to the long ballads and epic-like folksongs that are a part of his repertoire. But he is not so impressed by the content of modern popular song, which he thinks is thin and somewhat silly. Even so, Paulie feels that the ascendency of the short song was inevitable:

> You know, I think them old people had a lot
> on their minds remembering all of those long
> songs. . .They had an awful lot on their minds
> . . .I think that was why so many of them
> people used to become "mental."

Mental illness a result of memorizing the complex texts of song: a sad commentary on the role of folklore, but one that Hall believes. And he, like many beyond Newfoundland's shores, feels that TV and radio are relaxing, personal, and easy means of entertainment.

It is not an accident that song makers such as Paul Hall have disappeared at the time when mass media have made their inroads into the life of all the peoples of the world; cultural space is limited, and under the power and prestige of the new media, the local voices of creativity have less and less meaning. It is sad irony that as the artists of the earth's "little traditions" lose their value to their own audiences, only then do they grow important to the outside world that will never hear them sing. And there is a desperate importance in saving and understanding the processes of creativity, wherever they may be found. Art as product is never valuable; only inside the matrix of society and within the heart of the human community does imagination serve its function. And this is where we must seek it.

NOTES

[1] Some of the material used in this paper was collected during the author's tenure as a Research Fellow at the Institute of Social and Economic Research, Memorial University of Newfoundland, for which grateful acknowledgement is expressed. I am also indebted to Herbert Halpert, whose "Vitality of Tradition and Local Songs," *Journal of the International Folk Music Council* 3:35-40, 1951, first called attention to these problems; to Edward D. Ives; and to Frank Loveland for his important assistance. A substantially different version of this paper was given at the meetings of the American Folklore Society at Toronto, Canada, On November 19, 1967.

[2] There have been efforts that have pointed in the direction suggested here: Roger D. Abrahams, "Patterns of Structure and Role Relationships in the Child Ballad in the United States," *Journal of American Folklore* 79:488-492, 1966; Archie Green, "The Carter Family's 'Coal Miner's Blues,'" *Southern Folklore Quarterly* 25:226-237, 1961, and "Hillbilly Music: Source and Symbol," *Journal of American Folklore* 78:204-228. 1965; John Greenway, "Folksong as an Anthropological Province: the Anthropological Approach," in *A Good Tale and a Bonnie Tune*, Mody C. Boatright, Wilson M. Hudson, and Allen Maxwell, eds., (Dallas, 1964), pp. 209-217, and "Folksongs as Socio-Historical Documents," *Western Folklore* 19:1-9, 1960; A. L. Lloyd, *The Singing Englishman*, (London, n.d.), and *Folk Song in England*, (New York, 1967); Alan Lomax, *The Folk Songs of North America in the English Language*, New York, 1960); John Messenger, "Anthropologist at Play: The Research Implications of Balladmongering," *American Anthropologist* 66:407-416, 1964; William E. Sellers, "Kinship in the British Ballads: The Historical Evidence," *Southern Quarterly* 20:199-215, 1956, and "Kindred and Clan in the Scottish Border Ballads," *Boston University Studies in English* 3:1-11, 1957; and Lowry C. Wimberly, *Folklore in the English and Scottish Ballads*, (Chicago, 1928).

[3] Alan Lomax, "Special Features of the Sung Communication," in *Essays on the Verbal and Visual Arts: Proceedings of the 1966 Annual Spring Meeting of the American Ethnogolical Society,* June Helm, ed., (Seattle, 1967), pp. 109-127.

[4] See John F. Szwed, *Public Culture and Private Imagery: Interpersonal Relations in a Newfoundland Peasant Society,* Newfoundland Social and Economic Studies No. 2, (St. John's, Newfoundland, 1966).

[5] William Doerflinger, *Shantymen and Shantyboys: Songs of the Sailor and Lumberman* (New York, 1951), p. 253.

[6] Doerflinger, ibid,; Edward D. Ives, "Satirical Songs in Maine and the Maritime Provinces of Canada," *Journal of the International Folk Music Council* 14:65-69, 1962; Edward D. Ives, *Larry Gorman: The Man Who Made the Songs,* (Bloomington, 1964); and Frank Rickaby, *Ballads and Songs of the Shanty-boy,* (Cambridge, Mass., 1926).

[7] For samples of Newfoundland satirical songs see *The Ryans and the Pittmans, The Kelligrew's Soiree,* and *Two Jinkers,* in Gerald S. Doyle, *Old-Time Songs and Poetry of Newfoundland* (St. John's, 1966), pp. 27, 32-33, 39; and *The Moonshine Can* in Omar Blondahl, *Newfoundlanders, Sing!: A Collection of Favorite Newfoundland Folk Songs,* (St. John's, 1964), pp. 25-26.

[8] Ives, *Larry Gorman* . . . , p. 184.

[9] Melville Jacobs, "Titles in an Oral Literature," *Journal of American Folklore* 70:157-172, 1957; and Dell Hymes, "Myths and Tale Titles of the Lower Chinook," *Journal of American Folklore* 70:139-145, 1959.

[10] James Faris, *Cat Harbour: A Newfoundland Fishing Settlement,* Newfoundland Social and Economic Studies, No. 3 (St. John's, Newfoundland, 1966), p. 103.

[11] George M. Foster, "Community Development and the Image of the Static Economy," *Community Development Bulletin* 12: 124-128, 1961, and "Peasant Society and the Image of Limited Good," *American Anthropoligist* 67:293-315,1965.

[12] Eric R. Wolf, "Types of Latin American Peasantry: A Preliminary Discussion," *American Anthropologist* 57:452-471, 1955; George M. Foster, "Interpersonal Relations in Peasant Society," *Human Organization* 19:178-180, 1960-1961; Edward C. Banfield, *The Moral Basis of a Backward Society,* (Glencoe, Ill., 1958); and S. C. Dube, *Indian Village,* (Ithaca, 1959).

[13] Timothy D. Murphy, "Back-Biting and Petty Bickering in an Irish Peasant Community: A Variation on Foster's Model," unpublished ms., 1965, p. 1.

[14] Ives, *Larry Gorman.* . . , pp. 20-22. For songs of similar intent, see those of these closely allied families: *A Married Woman's Lament* (Sigmund Spaeth, *Read 'Em and Weap* (Garden City, 1935), pp. 26-27); *Bachelor's Lament* (John Harrington Cox, *Folk-Songs of the South* (Cambridge; 1925), p. 160); *Old Bachelor* (Vance Randolph, *Ozark Folksongs* (Columbia, Missouri, 1949), v. III, pp. 62-63); *Bachelor's Hall* (Dorothy Scarborough, *From a Southern Porch* (N.Y., 1919), p. 165); *When I Was a Young Man* (Mary O. Eddy, *Ballads and Songs from Ohio* (Hatboro, 1964), pp. 181-183); *I Wish I Was Single Again* (Vance Randolph, *Ozark Folksongs,* pp. 66-69).

THE AUTHORS

Henry Glassie is former Editor of *Keystone Folklore Quarterly* and author of (among numerous things) *Pattern in the Material Folk Culture of the Eastern United States.* He is a member of the faculty of the Folklore Institute, Indiana University.

Edward D. Ives is the author of *Larry Gorman: The Man Who Made the Songs* and numerous other works. He is Professor of Folklore in the Department of Anthropology, University of Maine.

John F. Szwed is the author of *Black America* and co-editor of *Afro-American Anthropology: Contemporary Perspectives.* He is with the Center for Urban Ethnography, University of Pennsylvania.

www.ingramcontent.com/pod-product-compliance
Lightning Source LLC
Chambersburg PA
CBHW032257150426
43195CB00008BA/482